BRITISH/COMMONWEALTH CRUISER

vs

ITALIAN CRUISER

The Mediterranean 1941–43

T0283642

ANGUS KONSTAM

OSPREY PUBLISHING
Bloomsbury Publishing Plc
Kemp House, Chawley Park, Cumnor Hill, Oxford OX2 9PH, UK
29 Earlsfort Terrace, Dublin 2, Ireland
1385 Broadway, 5th Floor, New York, NY 10018, USA
E-mail: info@ospreypublishing.com
www.ospreypublishing.com

OSPREY is a trademark of Osprey Publishing Ltd

First published in Great Britain in 2022

© Osprey Publishing Ltd, 2022

All rights reserved. No part of this publication may be reproduced or
transmitted in any form or by any means, electronic or mechanical, including
photocopying, recording, or any information storage or retrieval system,
without prior permission in writing from the publishers.

A catalogue record for this book is available from the British Library.

ISBN: PB 9781472849687; eBook 9781472849694; ePDF 9781472849700;
XML 9781472849717

22 23 24 25 26   10 9 8 7 6 5 4 3 2 1

Maps by Bounford.com
Colour artwork illustrations by Ian Palmer
Index by Alison Worthington
Typeset by PDQ Digital Media Solutions, Bungay, UK
Printed and bound in India by Replika Press Private Ltd.

Photographs
The photographic images that appear in this work are from the Stratford
Archive, unless otherwise indicated.

Osprey Publishing supports the Woodland Trust, the UK's leading woodland
conservation charity.

To find out more about our authors and books visit
www.ospreypublishing.com. Here you will find extracts, author interviews,
details of forthcoming events and the option to sign up for our newsletter.

A note on measure
Both Imperial and metric measurements have been used in this book.
Conversion tables are provided below:

1in. = 2.54cm
1ft = 0.3m
1yd = 0.9m
1 mile = 1.6km
1lb = 0.45kg
1 long ton = 1.02 metric tonnes

1mm = 0.039in.
1cm= 0.39in.
1m = 1.09yd
1km = 0.62 miles
1kg = 2.2lb
1 metric tonne = 0.98 long tons

Acronyms and abbreviations

AFCT	Admiralty Fire Control Table
AA	anti-aircraft
AP	armour-piercing
CLAA	anti-aircraft light cruiser
CPBC	common pointed ballistic cap
DCT	director control tower
DP	dual purpose
HACS	High Angle Control System
HA	high-angle
HE	high explosive (see SAPC)
mps	metres per second
PPI	plan position indicator
SAPC	semi-armour-piercing common (see HE)

Title page photograph: HMS *Euryalus*, a Dido-class cruiser.

Front cover (above): HMS *Naiad*, a Dido-class light anti-aircraft cruiser
designed to fill the Royal Navy's growing need for adequate fleet protection
from enemy aircraft. (Ian Palmer)
Front cover (below): RM *Raimondo Montecuccoli*, one of two Italian ships in
the Montecuccoli class. These vessels comprised the third batch of
Condottiere-type light cruisers to be built. (Ian Palmer)

CONTENTS

Introduction   4

Chronology   6

Design and Development   8

The Strategic Situation   35

Technical Specifications   43

The Combatants   53

Combat   63

Analysis   73

Aftermath   76

Bibliography   78

Index   80

INTRODUCTION

On 10 June 1940, when Italy entered World War II, the Royal Navy was already overstretched. Norway and Denmark had been overrun, and the battle for France was in its final throes. In British waters the Home Fleet had played its part in the defence of Norway, but it was powerless to intervene in the disastrous campaign in France and the Low Countries. While all this had been taking place, the British Mediterranean Fleet had been passively awaiting developments. In peacetime its primary task was to protect the sea route which stretched for 1,900 nautical miles, from Port Said – the northern end of the Suez Canal – in the east, to Gibraltar in the west. It had three naval bases in the Mediterranean, at Alexandria in Egypt, Gibraltar and the fortress island of Malta, midway between the two. Any future war in the Mediterranean would centre around the protection of this vital sea route, and with it the maritime link between these three bases.

For the Regia Marina (the Italian Navy), its overall strategy was influenced by three main factors: geography, naval strength and Italy's military commitments. The Italian peninsula lies roughly midway between Gibraltar and the Suez Canal, and so the Italian fleet was well placed to interdict the British sea route between the two. The naval base at Taranto in the 'heel' of Italy lies close to this sea lane, and less than 500 nautical miles from the shores of North Africa. The coast there formed part of the Italian colony of Libya, which was bordered to the west by the French colonies of Tunisia and Algeria, while to the east lay Egypt, a country under British protection. So, while the Italians would attempt to sever Britain's trans-Mediterranean sea lane, they also had to maintain their own sea links with Libya. As the war progressed, Italy also began military operations in Greece, which meant another Italian sea route would need to be protected.

At the halfway point along Britain's trans-Mediterranean sea route was the island of Malta. It also lay close to Italy's sea route between the Italian mainland and its

This depiction of the Regia Marina *Colleoni* captures the sleek, graceful lines of all the Condottiere group of Italian light cruisers. She was the last of the da Giussano class to enter service, eight years before she went to war, and the first of them to be lost. On 19 July 1940 the *Bartolomeo Colleoni* was sunk off Cape Spada in north-west Crete by the Australian cruiser *Sydney*, accompanied by a flotilla of destroyers.

Libyan colony. So, the island became the focal point of the campaign. In British hands, it represented a haven midway along its sea route, while it also represented a major threat to Italy's links with Libya. Safeguarding Malta and keeping the island supplied and protected became a major commitment for Britain as the war went on. For the most part, this meant ensuring convoys reached the island from Gibraltar. To counter them, the Italians made full use of their air bases in Sardinia and Sicily, forcing the Malta convoys to run a gauntlet of air attacks, while the Italian Navy was also increasingly committed to attacking these convoys. So, too, was the German Luftwaffe (Air Force); its intervention in the campaign would significantly tip the naval balance in the region.

Generally speaking, the two rival battle fleets were used to counter each other, and to support other naval operations, rather than as the arbiter of victory in the theatre. Therefore, the task of protecting or threatening the two rival sea routes fell to lighter naval forces, to submarines and to aircraft. In 1798, during another naval campaign in the Mediterranean, Horatio Nelson famously exclaimed: 'Frigates! Were I to die at this moment, want of frigates would be found engraved on my heart.' Almost a century and a half later, his successor, Andrew Cunningham, might well have uttered a similar sentiment, only with the word 'frigates' replaced by 'cruisers'.

While destroyers were the vital workhorses of both the British and Italian fleets, it was the cruiser that would become the key type of surface warship in the naval battle for the Mediterranean. This is particularly true of the light cruiser, as heavy cruisers were usually required to operate with the battle fleet. Light cruisers were fast and powerful enough to threaten enemy convoys, and to protect friendly ones. When called on, they were also able to support the rival battle fleets. Other wartime roles included serving as makeshift troop transports and bombarding the enemy coast. It was the sheer versatility of these cruisers that made them such an indispensible part of their fleets. The aim of this book is not to outline the whole course of the naval battle for the Mediterranean. Instead, by concentrating on the activities of the rival cruisers, we can gain a more focused insight into the way this bitterly contested campaign was fought.

CHRONOLOGY

1940

10 June Italy declares war on Britain and France.

25 June First Italian convoy bound for Libya sails from Naples.

28 June British cruisers sink Italian destroyer *Espero*.

9 July Battle of Calabria (Punta Stilo) – indecisive clash of battle fleets.

19 July Engagement off Cape Spada, Crete – light cruiser *Bartolomeo Colleoni* sunk by *Sydney*.

12 October *Ajax* attacks Italian convoy in Ionian Sea, sinking a destroyer and two torpedo boats.

11 November Fleet Air Arm attack on the Italian battle fleet at Taranto – three battleships damaged.

27 November Battle of Cape Spartivento (Teulada) – indecisive clash between battle fleets.

18 December Two Italian cruisers bombard Greek army positions on Corfu.

1941

6–14 January Operation *Excess* – major British attempt to ship supplies to Malta.

9 February Force H bombards Genoa, while Italian battle fleet fails to intercept it.

26 March Heavy cruiser *York* torpedoed and sunk by Italian motor boats in Suda Bay, Crete.

27–29 March Battle of Cape Matapan – Allied victory – three Italian heavy cruisers sunk.

31 March AA cruiser *Bonaventure* sunk off Crete by Italian submarine.

16 April Engagement off the Kerkennah Bank (Battle of the Buoys).

27 April Athens falls to the Axis.

20 May Commencement of Operation *Mercury* – the Axis invasion of Crete.

21–22 May Royal Navy attempts to intercept Axis convoys – two British light cruisers sunk.

28 May–1 June Naval evacuation of troops from Crete – one light cruiser sunk and three damaged.

22 June Commencement of Operation *Barbarossa* – the Axis invasion of the Soviet Union.

22 July Operation *Substance* – the first major convoy operation to resupply beleaguered Malta.

24 September Operation *Halberd* – a major Malta convoy operation.

21 October Force K formed in Malta, from two light cruisers and two destroyers.

9 November Battle of the Duisburg (or Beta) convoy, fought off Calabria – a victory for Force K.

13 December Italian light cruisers *da Barbiano* and *da Giussano* sunk off Cape Bon.

14 December Light cruiser *Galatea* sunk by German U-boat.

17 December First Battle of Sirte – indecisive clash between two groups of convoy escorts.

18 December Force K runs into minefield off Tripoli – *Neptune* sunk and two cruisers damaged.

1942

22 March	Second Battle of Sirte – minor defensive victory in defence of an Allied convoy.
11 May	Three British destroyers sunk off Benghazi by German aircraft.
12–15 June	Operations *Harpoon* and *Vigorous* – a two-pronged and costly Malta convoy operation.
15 June	Battle of Pantelleria – attack on Malta convoy by Italian cruisers and destroyers.
1–27 July	First Battle of El Alamein – Rommel's drive into Egypt halted.
10–14 August	Operation *Pedestal* – the largest Malta convoy operation of the war.
23 October–1 November	Second Battle of El Alamein – decisive defeat of Axis forces in North Africa.
8–16 November	Operation *Torch* – Allied landings in French-occupied Morocco and Algeria.
11 November	Beginning of Tunisian campaign as Allied forces enter Tunisia from the west.

1943

29 January	British Eighth Army enters Tunisia.
10 April	Heavy cruiser *Trieste* sunk by US air raid on La Maddalena.
7 May	Allies enter Tunis.
13 May	Axis resistance in North Africa ends.
10 June	Operation *Husky* – Allied landings in Sicily.
17 July	Clash in Strait of Messina.
25 July	Collapse of Mussolini's Italian government.
6–8 August	Attempted sorties from La Spezia by Italian cruisers thwarted by Allied airpower.
8 September	Temporary armistice between Italy and Allies – Germans seize any Italian warships they can.
9 September	Operation *Avalanche* – Allied landings at Salerno on Italian mainland.
9–11 September	Italian battle fleet sails to Malta for internment – battleship *Roma* is sunk by Germans.
23 September	Foundation of breakaway Italian Republic, governed by Mussolini.
29 September	Long Armistice signed off Malta.
13 October	Kingdom of Italy declares war on Germany.

The Southampton-class light cruiser *Gloucester*, in a remarkable picture taken from a German Ju-87 Stuka dive bomber. On 22 May the cruiser sank in the Antikithera Channel off Crete after being hit repeatedly in a relentless succession of attacks by Luftwaffe dive-bombers.

DESIGN AND DEVELOPMENT

THE BRITISH CRUISER FLEET

During World War I, Britain concentrated on building small light cruisers armed with 6in. guns, designed primarily for operations in the North Sea. A total of 44 of these warships were built during the war, and many of these would still be in service in 1940. The best of them, and those which survived the interwar years, were the so-called C-class cruisers, which were actually a group of similarly designed cruisers divided into several smaller classes (Caledon, Ceres and Carlisle), as well as the D-class cruisers which entered service during the closing months of World War I. The two E-class cruisers laid down at the same time didn't enter service until 1926.

By then though, Britain had already begun building a class of three larger Hawkins-class cruisers, designed for ocean cruising, and armed with 7.5in. guns. While these weren't particularly innovative ships, their construction had an influence on the disarmament negotiations, which led to the Washington Naval Treaty of 1922. Effectively, these large, well-armed cruisers led to their accommodation in the treaty ceiling for cruisers, of a 10,000-ton displacement and a maximum gun calibre of 8in. From that point on, until 1930, all British interwar cruisers would be built to conform to this ceiling. Also, as the treaty never specified a maximum number of these large cruisers, the major naval powers embarked on what was essentially a cruiser race.

Concerns about the sustainability of this race led to a call for further international discussions. The result was the London Naval Treaty of 1930, which not only limited the number of cruisers each maritime power could have, but also recognized two different types of cruiser. The 8in. 'treaty cruisers' built to conform to the Washington treaty limits formed one category, which unofficially came to be labelled the 'heavy cruisers'. These were now distinct from cruisers with a gun calibre of up to 6.1in., which became known as 'light cruisers'. So, Britain's wartime C, D and E classes were now deemed light cruisers, while the Hawkins class, with their 7.5.in guns, became heavy cruisers. From that point on, Britain's naval shipbuilding programme concentrated on the production of light cruisers, which gradually came to outnumber the heavy cruisers in the fleet.

THE HEAVY CRUISERS

During the war, the three Hawkins-class cruisers were ordered to counter the threat posed by German ocean raiders. However, all but one of them entered service after the war was over. Even then, the first of these, *Cavendish*, was converted into the aircraft carrier *Vindictive* while still under construction. She would eventually be rebuilt as a cruiser. These were long, elegant ships, carrying their 7.5in. guns in seven single mounts. Their armoured belt was up to 3in. thick, which gave them a modicum of protection, but they could only make just under 30 knots. When the war began in September 1939 *Hawkins*, *Frobisher* and *Effingham* were still in service, albeit held in the mothballed reserve fleet. Although all three were brought into active service, none of them was deployed in the Mediterranean. The real importance of the Hawkins class was that, thanks to British influence at the Washington naval conference, it set the yardstick for the treaty cruisers which followed.

The Washington Treaty led directly to the design of the treaty cruiser – warships built to conform to the treaty ceiling on gun calibre and displacement. For the Royal Navy, this helped fill a specific need. Until the late 1920s, the vessels of the Hawkins class were the only cruisers in the fleet specifically designed to protect Britain's sea trade routes. There was a real need for ocean-going cruisers with the range to patrol the world's oceans, and to safeguard British shipping lanes in times of war. The British Admiralty also realized that a consequence of the treaty was that other naval powers would immediately begin building treaty cruisers. So, it planned to build its own heavy cruiser force, while also making sure these new warships were able to fulfil this vital global role.

Kent class	
Kent class (5) *Berwick*, *Cornwall*, *Cumberland*, *Kent*, *Suffolk* *Berwick* and *Kent* deployed in Mediterranean, 1940–41	
In service	1928
Displacement	13,400–13,540 tons
Dimensions	Length: 630–633ft; Beam: 68ft 4in.; Draught: 20ft 6in.
Propulsion	Four shafts, powered by four turbines and eight boilers, generating 80,000shp
Maximum speed	31½ knots

Armament	Eight 8in. guns in four twin turrets, eight (four in Kent) 4in. QF Mk XIX AA guns in twin mounts, sixteen 2pdr pom-pom AA guns in eight-barrelled mounts, eight 21in. torpedo tubes in two quadruple mounts
Armour	Main Belt: 1–4in. (2.5–10.2cm); Turrets: 1in. (2.5cm)
Sensors	Type 273, Type 281, Type 284 radar, Type 132 sonar
Aircraft	Single catapult mounted amidships, one Supermarine Walrus float plane
Complement	685–710

This meant that its own treaty cruisers would have to be extremely seaworthy, be reasonably speedy and have a good cruising range. Various designs were considered, and it soon became obvious that in order to keep the displacement within treaty limits, these ships had to be relatively lightly armoured. In 1924 a plan was approved, and later that year the first of five ships of the Kent class were laid down. They were named after English counties or boroughs; *Berwick, Cornwall, Cumberland, Kent* and *Suffolk*. These carried eight 8in. guns in four twin turrets, and were capable of making just over 31 knots. This though, was achieved by reducing the armoured belt to a protective box over the engine spaces and magazines up to 4.4in. thick, but which tapered to just 1in. at the ends. The ships' hulls were high, to improve seakeeping qualities, and they could carry enough fuel oil to give them a range of 9,350 nautical miles.

The five Kent-class cruisers were launched in 1926, and completed from 1926–27. These, though, were only the first of several classes of similar cruisers. As early as 1925–26 another class of four cruisers was ordered. These ships (*Devonshire, London, Shropshire* and *Sussex*) were laid down in 1926–27 and became the London class, which were little more than improved versions of the Kents. They had the same protected scheme, but omitted the anti-torpedo bulges fitted to the Kents. This increased the ships' speed at the expense of underwater protection. The ships were a little longer too, which meant the forecastle was extended to improve seakeeping qualities, and there was more internal space. These all entered service in 1929.

The last of this County batch of cruisers were the two ships of the Norfolk class, which were laid down in 1927. These were essentially repeats of the London class, but they mounted an improved version of the 8in. turret, and minor improvements were made in the protective scheme, which added a little to the displacement. *Dorsetshire* and *Norfolk* were laid down in 1927, and completed three years later. They were expensive ships, and so in 1926 plans were approved for a slightly smaller version of these treaty cruisers. The first of these was *York*, a one-ship class, which was built at the same time as the Norfolks. She was similarly designed, but only mounted three twin 8in. gun turrets. She also had a lower freeboard amidships and aft, and was further distinguished by only having two rather than three funnels. This in turn allowed her armour to be increased slightly.

Like her near-sister *Exeter*, the British heavy cruiser *York* only mounted six 8in. guns, which limited her effectiveness. Still, from late 1940 she proved a useful member of the Mediterranean Fleet, seeing action off Cape Passero that October. She was crippled by Italian MAS boats in Crete's Suda Bay the following March.

York class	
Ships in class (1): *York* Deployed in Mediterranean, 1940–41	
In service	1930
Displacement	10,350 tons (deep load)
Dimensions	Length: 575ft; Beam: 57ft; Draught: 20ft 3in.
Propulsion	Four shafts, powered by four turbines and eight boilers, generating 80,000shp
Maximum speed	32 knots
Armament	Six 8in./50 (20.3cm) Mk VIII guns in three twin turrets, four 4in./45 QF Mk V AA guns in single mounts, eight 0.5mm machine guns in two quadruple mounts, six 21in. torpedo tubes in two triple mounts
Armour	Main Belt: 1–4in.; Turrets: 1in.
Sensors	Type 132 sonar
Aircraft	Single catapult mounted amidships, one Supermarine Walrus float plane
Complement	623

A near-sister was *Exeter*, another one-ship class. Originally designed as a sister to *York*, she was modified sufficiently by the addition of a little more armoured protection that she eventually constituted her own class. Both *York* and *Exeter* carried six 8in. guns, in three twin turrets. *Exeter*, though, turned out to be the last of the Royal Navy's treaty cruisers. By the time she was completed in the summer of 1931, Britain as well as Italy was a signatory to the London Naval Treaty (1930). The treaty limited the number of heavy cruisers a country could have. Britain's quota was 15, which it would exceed by one when *York* and *Exeter* entered service. So, some of the Hawkins class were mothballed. However, there would be no limit on the numbers of light cruisers in the fleet. So, from 1930 on, the building of heavy cruisers was abandoned in favour of light cruisers mounting 6in. guns. Incidentally, the Italian government never signed the treaty, but followed a similar shipbuilding course to that of the signatory nations.

THE LIGHT CRUISERS

The London treaty imposed a 10,000-ton displacement ceiling for all new 6in. cruisers. Britain already had several of these lighter-armed cruisers still in service, of the C, D and E classes. It was clear, though, that more modern replacements were needed. This led directly to the drawing up of plans for the Leander class. These were intended to be used primarily for commerce protection – guarding sea lanes, escorting convoys and hunting down ocean raiders. The design was developed from plans of the *York*, but these would be distinguished by having a single funnel – the first British cruisers with one funnel since the Victorian era. They would be armed with eight 6in. guns in four twin turrets, augmented by quick-firing 4in. guns, torpedo tubes and provision for a float plane. In all, five of them would be built (*Achilles*, *Ajax*, *Leander*, *Neptune* and *Orion*), while three two-funnelled and slightly modified versions were

In June 1940 *Sydney*, commanded by Captain John Collins RAN, formed part of Rear Admiral Tovey's 7th Cruiser Squadron. That summer, she bombarded Italian positions at Bardia, finished off the Italian destroyer *Espero*, and took part in the Battle of Calabria. Then, on 19 July, off Cape Spada, she sank the Italian cruiser *Bartolomeo Colleoni*, and damaged *Bande Nere*. Later that year, *Sydney* would be in action again in the Strait of Otranto. She remained with the Mediterranean Fleet until the following January, when she returned home for a refit. *Sydney* remained in home waters until she was sunk in action with the German raider *Kormoran* on 19 November 1941.

built for the Royal Australian Navy (*Hobart*, *Perth* and *Sydney*). Seven of these ships would see service in the Mediterranean.

Leander class	
Ships in class (5): *Achilles*, *Ajax*, *Leander*, *Neptune*, *Orion* All but *Achilles* deployed in Mediterranean at various times	
In service	1933–34
Displacement	9,000–9,280 tons (deep load)
Dimensions	Length: 554ft 6in.; Beam: 55ft 2in.–15ft 8in.; Draught: 19ft–19ft 8in.
Propulsion	Four shafts, powered by four turbines and six boilers, generating 72,000shp
Maximum speed	32½ knots
Armament	Eight 6in./50 Mk XXIII guns in four twin turrets, eight 4in./45 QF Mk XVI AA guns in twin mounts (*Achilles* carried four 4in./45 QF Mk V AA guns in single mounts), eight 21in. torpedo tubes in two quadruple mounts.
Armour	Main Belt: 1–3.5in.; Turrets: 1in.
Sensors	Type 128 sonar
Aircraft	Single catapult mounted amidships, one Fairey Seafox float plane
Complement	570
Notes	These cruisers were all modified during service. In early 1941, *Ajax*, *Leander* and *Orion* had their catapult and aircraft removed, while *Neptune* received six quadruple machine guns and three single 2pdr pom-poms, as well as Type 281, 284 and 285 radars. At the same time, *Ajax* received a Type 279 set, while *Orion* was fitted with Type 284, 279 and 285 radars later that year.

In November 1941 the Leander-class light cruiser *Neptune* became part of Force K, based in Malta. However, on 19 December she ran into an Italian minefield off Benghazi, and sank with the loss of all but one of her crew.

Perth class	
Ships in class (3): *Hobart*, *Perth*, *Sydney* – all Royal Australian Navy All deployed in Mediterranean at various times	
In service	1935–36
Displacement	8,850–9,150 tons (deep load)
Dimensions	Length: 562ft 3in.; Beam: 56ft 8in.; Draught: 18ft 6in.–19ft
Propulsion	Four shafts, powered by four turbines and four boilers, generating 72,000shp
Maximum speed	32½ knots
Armament	Eight 6in./50 Mk XXIII guns in four twin turrets, eight 4in./45 Mk XVI AA guns in twin mounts, twelve 0.5in. machine guns in quadruple mounts, six 21in. torpedo tubes in two triple mounts.
Armour	Main Belt: 1–3.5in.; Turrets: 1in.
Sensors	Type 128 sonar
Aircraft	Single catapult mounted amidships, one Fairey Seafox float plane
Complement	570
Notes	These cruisers were all modified during service. In mid-1941 *Perth* had her catapult extended to accommodate a Supermarine Walrus, and gained a Type 279 radar. In late 1941 *Hobart* gained eight 2pdr pom-poms in two quadruple mounts; a year later her catapult was removed, together with her machine guns, but she gained several radar and 20mm guns.

The *Arethusa*, namesake of her class. Financial constraints during the early 1930s led to the Arethusas being limited to three twin turrets, rather than the four turrets of the preceding Leander class. Still, they were well designed, and thanks to a better machinery layout they were slightly less vulnerable to damage than the Leanders.

By the time the Leanders were entering service in 1933, the first of the Arethusa class were being laid down. During this period many light cruiser designs were considered, and then modified in line with financial constraints. The four ships of the Arethusa class (*Arethusa*, *Galatea*, *Penelope* and *Aurora*) were the result of a reduced naval budget, and the determination of the Admiralty to build whatever kind of light cruisers it could afford. The result was a small 5,450-ton cruiser, armed with six 6in. guns in three twin turrets. Protection was limited to 3in. of armour over the magazines, but they had four propeller shafts, and could make just over 32 knots. They entered service between 1935 and 1937. All four would serve in the Mediterranean.

Arethusa class

Ships in class (4): *Arethusa*, *Aurora*, *Galatea*, *Penelope* All deployed in Mediterranean at various times	
In service	1935–37
Displacement	6,665–6,715 tons (deep load)
Dimensions	Length: 506ft; Beam: 51ft; Draught: 16ft 6in.
Propulsion	Four shafts, powered by four turbines and four boilers, generating 64,000shp
Maximum speed	32 knots
Armament	Six 6in./50 Mk XXIII guns in three twin turrets, eight 4in./45 QF Mk XVI AA guns in twin mounts (*Arethusa* carried four 4in./45 QF Mk V AA guns in single mounts), six 21in. torpedo tubes in two triple mounts.
Armour	Main Belt: 1–3in.; Turrets: 1in.
Sensors	Type 128 sonar
Aircraft	Single catapult mounted amidships (not *Aurora*), one Fairey Seafox float plane
Complement	500
Notes	These cruisers were all modified during service. In 1940, *Aurora* and *Galatea* gained eight 2pdr pom-poms in 2 quadruple mounts, while *Arethusa*, *Galatea* and *Penelope* had their catapults removed. During 1941–42 various radars were fitted to all ships, and additional 20mm AA guns were added.

During the early 1930s the British were keen to continue the drive to limit naval production by international treaties. Other nations, though, were less keen on these restrictions. The failure of the Geneva Conference in 1932 was followed by the limited success of the Second London Naval Treaty of 1936, when Japan and Italy withdrew from the talks, and Germany was already forging its own path. By then, the Admiralty was concerned that other naval powers were building larger and more powerful light cruisers than Britain. In 1933, plans were drawn up for a larger, better-armed and better-protected light cruiser, displacing up to 10,000 tons. The result was the highly successful Southampton class of eight light cruisers. These carried twelve 6in. guns in

The Southampton class was designed in response to the building of powerful Japanese light cruisers. The result was a cruiser type that surpassed the Admiralty's expectations in terms of excellent balance between firepower, speed and protection. However, *Southampton*, pictured here, was lost to air attack off Sicily in January 1942, while escorting a Malta convoy.

The Southampton-class light cruiser *Sheffield* joined Force H in Gibraltar in August 1940, and for the next 14 months she was deployed on operations in the Western Mediterranean, apart from her Atlantic sojourn in May 1941 to hunt the *Bismarck*. She finally left for home in October 1941.

four triple turrets, augmented by 4in. and 2pdr anti-aircraft guns, as well as torpedoes. With a 3½in belt, these ships were reasonably well protected, and they had a top speed of 32½ knots.

The first five of the Southamptons were laid down in 1934–35, and were completed in 1937. The last three (*Gloucester*, *Liverpool* and *Manchester*), laid down in 1936, are sometimes regarded as a separate class, as they incorporated modest improvements to the ships' protective scheme. All eight Southamptons saw service in the Mediterranean. In 1936, the Admiralty decided to build two similar cruisers, with a longer hull, a larger displacement and incorporating the improved armour of the *Gloucester* batch. These became the two-ship Edinburgh class (*Edinburgh* and *Belfast*), the latter being preserved as a historic ship, berthed in the Pool of London. Both of these cruisers entered service in 1939.

Southampton class	
Ships in class (8): *Birmingham, Glasgow, Gloucester, Liverpool, Manchester, Newcastle, Sheffield, Southampton* All deployed in Mediterranean at various times	
In service	1937
Displacement	11,350 tons (deep load)
Dimensions	Length: 591ft 6in.; Beam: 61ft 8in.; Draught: 20ft 4in.
Propulsion	Four shafts, powered by four turbines and four boilers, generating 75,000shp
Maximum speed	32 knots
Armament	Twelve 6in./50 Mk XXIII guns in four triple turrets, eight 4in./45 QF Mk XVI AA guns in twin mounts, eight 2pdr pom-poms in quadruple mounts, eight 0.5in. machine guns in quadruple mounts, six 21in. torpedo tubes in two triple mounts.
Armour	Main Belt: 1–4.5in.; Turrets: 1in.
Sensors	Type 79Y radar, Type 132 sonar
Aircraft	Single catapult mounted amidships, two Supermarine Walrus float planes
Complement	920
Notes	These cruisers were all modified during service. In 1940–41, most received radar, or improved sets, and several had their light anti-aircraft upgraded. This process continued for the surviving ships in 1942–43.

The light cruisers of the Fiji (or Colony) class were designed in line with the treaty restrictions of the Second London Naval Conference of 1936, which limited the displacement of new light cruisers to 8,000 tons. This meant that there would be no repeats of the Southampton and Edinburgh classes, which were being built as the treaty was signed. So, during 1937, various designs were considered for a more compact version, and these resulted in the eleven-ship Fiji class, which was laid down in 1938, and completed from 1940–42. The hull was shorter and narrower than the earlier cruisers, and had a square-off transom stern.

Unlike most of their counterparts in other navies, the bridges of almost all British and Commonwealth cruisers were open to the elements. This shows the compass platform of the light cruiser *Sheffield*. It was from here that the captain commanded the ship when it went into action.

Fiji class

Ships in class (11): *Bermuda, Ceylon, Fiji, Gambia, Jamaica, Kenya, Mauritius, Newfoundland, Nigeria, Trinidad, Uganda*
All but *Trinidad, Gambia* and *Bermuda* deployed in Mediterranean at various times

In service	1940–43
Displacement	10,830–11,090 tons (deep load)
Dimensions	Length: 555ft 6in.; Beam: 62ft ; Draught: 19ft 10in.
Propulsion	Four shafts, powered by four turbines and four boilers, generating 72,500shp
Maximum speed	31½ knots
Armament	Twelve 6in./50 Mk XXIII guns in four triple turrets (nine guns in three turrets in Ceylon, Newfoundland and Uganda), eight 4in./45 QF Mk XVI AA guns in twin mounts, eight 2pdr pom-poms in quadruple mounts (twelve in three mounts in Ceylon, Newfoundland and Uganda), six 21in. torpedo tubes in two triple mounts.
Armour	Main Belt: 3.25–3.5in.; Turrets: 1–2in.
Sensors	Type 281 radar, Type 132 sonar
Aircraft	Single catapult mounted amidships, two Supermarine Walrus float planes
Complement	920
Notes	These cruisers were all modified during service. In 1941, *Fiji* gained a Type 284 radar and an extra quad machine gun. Other ships received Type 273 and 284 radar and several 20mm AA guns during 1941–43.

The Fiji-class cruiser *Kenya* was commissioned in September 1940, and served with the Home Fleet until June 1942, apart from one brief Mediterranean foray. During Operation *Pedestal* in August she was torpedoed by the Italian submarine *Alagi*, but limped back to Gibraltar. Repairs lasted until the end of the year, but once back in service she never returned to the Mediterranean.

They carried the same armament as the Southamptons, as well as a similar protective system to the first ships of the earlier class. The Fijis had a lot crammed into their small hulls, but they were still effective and powerful warships. Three more (*Uganda*, *Newfoundland* and *Ceylon*) were laid down in 1939, and they joined the fleet in 1943. These, though, were modified by losing an after turret, in exchange for an improved anti-aircraft armament. This Uganda batch is sometimes treated as a separate class in its own right. Other wartime light cruisers would follow, including two Swiftsure class variants of the modified (or Uganda) Fijis, with a wider beam and an improved anti-aircraft armament. Finally, the Tiger class, laid down during the war, were still incomplete when the war ended. Apart from these later classes, most of the British and Commonwealth light cruiser force was heavily committed to the Mediterranean campaign, and consequently it suffered several losses to enemy submarines and aircraft. Without them, though, the campaign would have taken a very different course.

THE AA CRUISERS

During the 1930s it was clear that in time of war, warships now faced an increased risk of attack from the air. The capabilities of modern aircraft were developing too rapidly to be ignored. The Admiralty's initial response was to increase the anti-aircraft provision for the fleet, and to build in more provision for anti-aircraft weapons for ships still being designed or built. Its key development around this time was the High Angle Control System (HACS), an anti-aircraft fire control device that calculated deflection, making fire far more accurate. By 1940, this dustbin-shaped device was installed on all British cruisers. In addition, high-angle (HA) guns were installed in cruisers as their secondary battery, which, as the name suggests, had the elevation to lay down effectively a barrage in front of high-

The Dido-class AA light cruiser *Naiad* under air attack while protecting a Malta convoy in May 1941. As flagship of the 15th Cruiser Squadron, she subsequently steamed east to play her part in the naval battles of Crete, and then spent much of her time supporting westbound Malta convoys. Her luck came to an end though on 11 March 1942, when she was torpedoed and sunk by *U-565* off the Egyptian coast.

flying aircraft. These were augmented by lighter 2pdr pom-poms, and multiple machine-gun mounts for close-range defence.

However, this wasn't enough. The Admiralty realized that it needed to do more than defend individual warships. There was also a need to provide anti-aircraft cover for fleet defence, and for the protection of convoys. The solution was to develop the anti-aircraft light cruiser (CLAA). During the mid-1930s, the Arethusa-class light cruisers were just entering service. So, the Admiralty's design team set about adapting the Arethusa design to a purpose-built anti-aircraft ship. The basic premise was that the 6in. guns mounted in the Arethusas would be replaced by smaller dual-purpose (DP) quick-firing guns, which could engage aircraft and surface targets with equal effectiveness. Fortuitously, just such a weapon was available – the 5.25in./50 QF Mark I. First developed in 1935, it had an impressive anti-aircraft ceiling of 46,500ft at 70 degrees of elevation, and was also effective against surface targets.

This amalgam of cruiser and gun resulted in the Dido class of anti-aircraft cruisers. In all, eleven ships were built in four batches, being laid down between the summer of 1937 and late 1939. The first of them entered service in the summer of 1940. In theory, these ships carried ten 5.25in. guns in five twin turrets. However, production delays meant that sufficient guns weren't initially available, so five ships of the class (*Bonaventure*, *Phoebe*, *Dido*, *Scylla* and *Charybdis*) were completed with only four turrets, and two of these (*Scylla* and *Charybdis*) carried 4.5in. rather than 5.25in. guns. Another five Didos were due to be built, but this was delayed following the outbreak of war. When work finally began on them in late 1939, they had been modified to carry a reduced armament of eight 5.25in. guns in twin turrets. This last batch was referred to as the Modified Dido class, or sometimes the Bellona class. They all joined the fleet in late 1943 or early 1944.

The Dido class was designed to provide the fleet with good anti-aircraft protection, but the Didos soon proved their worth against surface targets too. *Euryalus*, pictured here, took part in most of the Malta convoy battles, as well as the First and Second Battles of Sirte.

The Dido class of light anti-
aircraft cruisers was designed to
fill the Royal Navy's growing need
for adequate fleet protection from
enemy aircraft. The Didos were
designed to carry the new 5.25in.
dual-purpose gun in a hull which
was essentially a modification of
the Arethusa class.
Naiad was built on Tyneside, and
entered service in July 1940.
After service with the Home Fleet,
she was sent to Gibraltar in April
1941, where she formed part of
Force H's escort of a Malta
convoy. Once there, she became
the flagship of Rear Admiral
King's 15th Cruiser Squadron. She
continued on to Crete, where in
May she took part in operations
against Axis invasion forces. The
following month she saw action
again, this time off Beirut,
fighting the Vichy French. For the
rest of the year she provided AA
cover for convoys in the Eastern
Mediterranean, and in December
she took part in the First Battle of
Sirte. She remained in the Eastern
Mediterranean, protecting
convoys and conducting sweeps
for enemy ones. However, on 11
March she was torpedoed and
sunk by *U-565* off the Egyptian
coast while returning to
Alexandria.

Dido class	
Ships in class (11): *Argonaut, Bonaventure, Charybdis, Cleopatra, Dido, Euryalus, Hermione, Naiad, Phoebe, Scylla, Sirius* All deployed in Mediterranean at various times	
In service	1940–42
Displacement	6,850–6,975 tons (deep load)
Dimensions	Length: 512ft; Beam: 50ft 6in.; Draught: 16ft 9in.
Propulsion	Four shafts, powered by four turbines and four boilers, generating 62,000shp
Maximum speed	32 knots
Armament	Eight or ten 5.25in./50 QF Mk I guns in four or five twin turrets (three turrets in *Bonaventure, Dido* and *Phoebe*, plus one 4in. Mk V starshell gun). Instead, *Charybdis* and *Scylla* carried eight 4.5in./45 QF Mk III guns in four twin turrets, plus in *Charybdis*, one single 4in. Mk V starshell gun; eight 2pdr pom-poms in quadruple mounts, six 21in. torpedo tubes in two triple mounts.
Armour	Main belt: 3in.
Sensors	Type 284, Type 279 radars, Type 128A sonar
Aircraft	None
Complement	530
Notes	These cruisers were all modified during service. During 1941–43, various radars were fitted to all ships, and additional 20mm AA guns were added.

The need for anti-aircraft cruisers was also filled by the conversion of existing warships. In the mid-1930s, two Ceres-class cruisers (*Coventry* and *Curlew*) were converted into anti-aircraft cruisers by replacing their 6in. guns with 4in. QF ones in single mounts. A third Ceres (*Curacao*) and three Carlisle-class cruisers (*Cairo, Calcutta* and *Capetown*) were also converted to an anti-aircraft role in 1938–40. The *Caledon*, namesake of her class, was also converted in 1942–43, as was the Carlisle-class cruiser *Colombo*. Several of these older anti-aircraft cruisers were deployed in the Mediterranean during the war, and *Cairo, Calcutta, Caradoc* and *Coventry* were lost in the theatre.

Carlisle class	
Ships in class (5): *Cairo, Calcutta, Capetown, Carlisle, Colombo* All deployed in Mediterranean at various times	
In service	1918–19. All but *Capetown* were converted into AA cruisers 1938–1943
Displacement	5,180–5,391 tons (deep load)
Dimensions	Length: 451ft 6in.; Beam: 43ft 6in.; Draught: 14ft 3in.
Propulsion	Two shafts, powered by two turbines and six boilers, generating 40,000shp

HMS NAIAD, MAY 1941

Italy's answer to the constraints
of the Washington Naval Treaty
(1922) was to design a treaty
cruiser, which dramatically
emphasized the need for speed
rather than protection. The result
was the two-ship Trento class, a
fast, elegant and well-armed pair
of cruisers which nevertheless
lacked sufficient armour to offer
much protection at all.
Trento, the namesake of the class,
entered service in 1929, and
spent the next decade showing
the flag around the world, or
serving as the flagship of the
Regia Marina's cruiser fleet. In
June 1940, as flagship of the 2nd
Division, she flew the flag of Rear
Admiral Cattaneo. The following
month she saw action at the
Battle of Calabria, and again in
November in the Battle of
Spartivento, when she formed
part of Rear Admiral Sansonetti's
3rd Division. She fought at
Matapan the following March, and
for the rest of 1941 she formed
part of the escort for the Libyan
convoys. During late 1941 and
early 1942 she saw action again
at the two Sirte battles, but on 15
June she was immobilized in a
bombing attack to the east of
Malta. The stricken cruiser was
finished off by the British
submarine Umbra.

Maximum speed	29½ knots
Armament	As completed: five 6in./45 Mk XII guns in single mounts, two 2pdr pom-poms in single mounts, eight 21in. torpedo tubes in two quadruple mounts. As converted: Eight 4in./45 Mk XVI QF guns in twin mounts, four 2pdr pom-poms in quadruple mounts, eight 0.5in. machine guns in quadruple mounts.
Armour	Main belt: 2.25–3in.
Sensors	Type 132 sonar, Type 272 (Type 279 in conversions) and Type 286 radars
Aircraft	None
Complement	334–400
Notes	These cruisers were all modified during service. All AA cruisers received extra 20mm AA guns during 1941–42, and Carlisle was given improved radar sets.

THE ITALIAN CRUISER FLEET

As a former Allied power in World War I, Italy was a signatory of the Washington Naval Treaty of 1922. In the treaty, Italy was given parity with France, but while the French began building new cruisers almost right away, the severe economic difficulties plaguing Italy meant that there was no money available to modernize the Regia Marina. Instead, after the war the naval budget was slashed. At the time, the main strength of the fleet lay in its four dreadnoughts, supplemented by an ageing collection of pre-war cruisers and destroyers. To make ends meet, the navy scrapped many of its older warships, or turned them into auxiliary vessels. This situation changed soon after the Fascist Party's march on Rome in October 1922, and the seizure of power by its leader Benito Mussolini. This change began modestly, with the approval in the 1922–23 budget for the design and building of the first of a new generation of modern Italian cruisers.

According to the treaty terms, new cruisers could only displace up to 10,000 tons, but could mount guns up to 8in. in calibre. The Italian naval architects intended their new warships to be treaty cruisers, conforming to these treaty restrictions. After building began, it became clear that these new ships would breach the treaty's displacement ceiling. Mussolini solved the problem by keeping this increase a secret. These cruisers were also built along unusual lines. Warship design involved achieving a balance between three elements – guns, armour and speed. If one element was increased, the other two would suffer in proportion. In the case of these new Trento-class cruisers, propulsive power was emphasized at the expense of protection. In effect, relatively thin armour meant that the weight saved could be used on her machinery. The result, though, was a pair of sleek, lightly protected cruisers which were some of the fastest ships of their kind.

In the next group, the Zara class, the balance was restored, and while four knots slower, these four cruisers boasted a protective belt of twice the thickness. A seventh

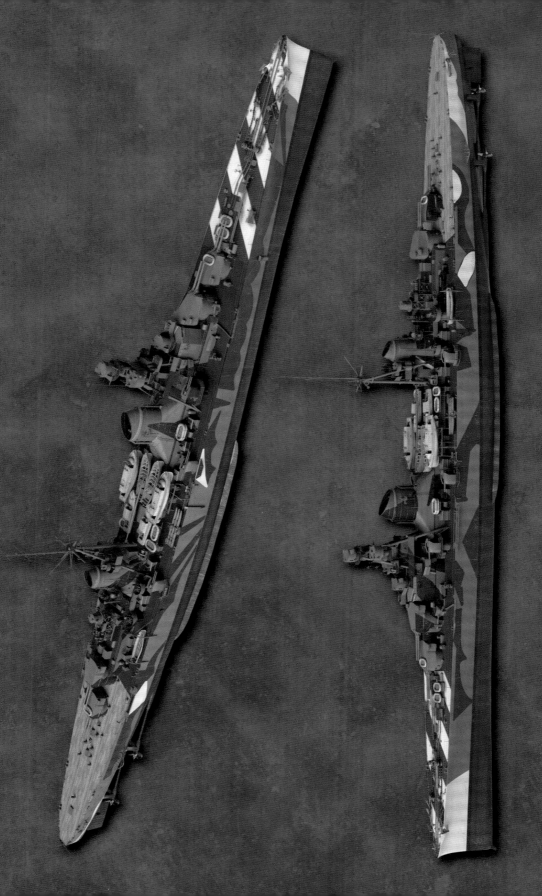

RM *TRENTO*, MARCH 1942

In July 1940, *Trento* saw action at the Battle of Calabria, and in November fought in the Battle of Spartivento as part of Rear Admiral Sansonetti's 3rd Division. She saw action at Matapan in March 1941, and again at the two Sirte battles, but in June she was immobilized in a bombing attack to the east of Malta before being finished off by the British submarine *Umbra*.

cruiser, the one-off *Bolzano*, saw a return to the Trento design, and so this fast cruiser was regarded as a half-sister of the earlier ships. All seven of these heavy cruisers were armed with eight 20.3cm (8in.) guns, mounted in four twin turrets, just like contemporary British treaty cruisers.

By the time the London Naval Treaty was negotiated in 1930, there had been a move away from these heavy 8in. cruisers. Instead, the major naval powers had edged towards a new smaller and cheaper design of light cruiser mounting 6in. guns. The Regia Marina followed suit, and so in the 1927–28 naval budget, the first of a new class of light cruisers was approved. These cruisers were primarily built to counter a new class of large and fast French destroyers, and so, like the Trentos, speed rather than protection was the priority. The first four of them formed the initial class of an evolving group of Italian light cruisers. As this first class was named after famous Italian *condottiere* ('mercenary captains'), this collection of what ultimately became six classes of cruisers was often collectively referred to as the Condottiere class. In fact, as each group differed, they each formed a warship class in their own right.

At the start of hostilities in June 1940, the Regia Marina boasted a powerful fleet of seven heavy cruisers and twelve light cruisers. In addition, plans had been drawn up for two more Condottieres, and work had begun on a new class of twelve small cruisers, the Capitani Romani class, which were designed as destroyer flotilla leaders. Of these, only three were completed in 1942–43, and only two of these saw limited active service. However, the other 19 cruisers saw extensive wartime service with the Regia Marina, and 13 of them were lost. This also highlighted another problem facing the Italian fleet. While it had a powerful navy, owing to Italy's limited shipbuilding capacity, the country would be hard put to replace any of these wartime losses.

THE HEAVY CRUISERS

The two ships of the Trento class were both fully fledged treaty cruisers, designed in 1923 to comply with the Washington Naval Treaty's terms. So, in an attempt to remain within the treaty's displacement ceiling, these cruisers were only lightly armoured, in order to carry the largest cruiser guns permitted, and to make the ships as fast as possible. This was an approach that matched the French Marine Nationale's Duquesne class, laid down in 1924–25, which also sported minimal armour. The Trento-class designs produced by Filippo Bonfiglietti called for a fairly conventional main gun layout, with four twin turrets – two forward and two aft. A secondary battery of dual-purpose and small anti-aircraft guns was augmented by torpedo tubes, and a catapult for a float plane. However, what set these cruisers apart was their speed. During trials they made almost 36 knots, five knots more than their official maximum speed.

The heavy cruiser *Zara*, namesake of her class, pictured firing her guns during a wartime exercise. During the war she served as the flagship of the 1st Division, flying the flag of Vice Admiral Carlo Cattaneo. After seeing extensive service, she was lost at the Battle of Matapan in March 1941.

Trento and Bolzano classes

Ships in Trento class (2): *Trento*, *Trieste*; ships in Bolzano class (1): *Bolzano*	
In service	1928–29 (*Bolzano* 1933)
Displacement	13,326–13,334 tons (deep load), *Bolzano*: 13,665 tons
Dimensions	Length: 196.96m, *Bolzano*: 196.9m; Beam: 20.6m; Draught: 6.8m, *Bolzano*: 6.8m
Propulsion	Four shafts, powered by four turbines and twelve boilers (ten boilers in *Bolzano*), generating 150,000shp
Maximum speed	36 knots
Armament	Eight 20.3cm/50 Mod 24 guns in four twin turrets (Mod 29 in *Bolzano*), sixteen 10cm/47 AA guns in twin mounts, four 40mm AA guns in single mounts, four 12.7mm machine guns in single mounts. *Bolzano*: eight 13.2mm machine guns in twin mounts, eight 53.3cm torpedo tubes in four twin mountings
Armour	Main belt: 7cm; Deck: 2–5cm; Turrets: 10cm; Conning tower: 4–10cm
Sensors	None
Aircraft	Single catapult mounted amidships, two Ro43 float planes
Complement	781, *Bolzano*: 725
Notes	During 1941–42, additional 20mm AA guns were added to the Trentos

The Zara class, which followed, represented a return to a more balanced design, but the *Bolzano*, ordered following approval of the 1929–30 naval budget, represented a return to the imbalance of the Trento class, where speed was emphasized over protection. The single-ship Bolzano class was in effect a half-sister of the Trentos, but she incorporated

In 1940 the Zara-class heavy cruiser *Fiume* formed part of the 1st Division, based at Taranto. She saw action at the Battle of Calabria (Punta Stilo) and then Cape Spartivento, when she traded salvos with the heavy cruiser *Berwick*. She was sunk at the Battle of Cape Matapan the following March, together with three other Italian heavy cruisers.

many of the improved design features incorporated into the Zara class. For instance, she had better watertight sub-division, the later cruisers' improved version of the Italian 20.3cm gun and improved stability. She was the last of the Regia Marina's treaty cruisers to enter service. By then, the emphasis had shifted to the production of lighter cruisers, armed with 15.2cm guns. So, *Bolzano* would be the last of the fleet's 8in. gun cruisers, which, when the smaller cruisers arrived, were rebranded as heavy cruisers.

In between the Trentos and the *Bolzano* came the Zara class. These, funded in the 1928–1931 naval budgets, were designed in 1928, while the Trentos were still on the stocks. They answered concerns about the lack of protection afforded to the earlier treaty cruisers, and so they represented a more balanced approach. The armoured belt was doubled to 15cm at its thickest point, but with only two propeller shafts, the new cruisers' propulsive power was less, giving them a top speed of 32 knots. The first two, *Zara* and *Fiume*, entered service in 1931, while *Gorizia* and *Pola* were commissioned the following year. In terms of all-round performance, these proved the best of Italy's treaty cruisers.

All seven of these heavy cruisers carried a respectable armament of eight 20.3cm guns, in four twin turrets. The turret design had its limitations, as did the lack of armour of three of the seven cruisers, but generally these ships proved useful additions to the Regia Marina. For the most part, they were formed into two cruiser divisions, and used to provide fast cover for convoys, or to form part of the main battle fleet. They suffered heavily though, and none of them would survive the war. *Fiume*, *Pola* and *Zara* were sunk at the Battle of Matapan in March 1941, *Trento* was torpedoed in June 1942, *Trieste* was lost in an air attack in April 1943 and then *Bolzano* and *Gorizia* were sunk in manned torpedo attacks in June 1944.

Zara class	
Ships in class (4): *Fiume*, *Gorizia*, *Pola*, *Zara*	
In service	1931–32
Displacement	13,994–14,330 tons (deep load)
Dimensions	Length: 182.8m; Beam: 20.62m; Draught: 7.2m
Propulsion	Two shafts, powered by two turbines and eight boilers, generating 95,000shp
Maximum speed	32 knots
Armament	Eight 20.3cm/53 Mod 29 guns in four twin turrets, sixteen 10cm/47 AA guns in twin mounts, four to six 40mm AA guns in single mounts, eight 13.2mm machine guns in four twin mounts
Armour	Main belt: 10–15cm; Deck: 2–7cm; Turrets: 12–15cm, Conning tower: 7–15cm
Sensors	None
Aircraft	Single catapult mounted forward, two Ro43 float planes
Complement	841
Notes	During 1942, *Gorizia* received four 37mm AA guns in twin mounts

THE LIGHT CRUISERS

The move to smaller lighter cruisers reflected two things. First, the navy felt it needed *grandi esploratori* ('grand scouts') – fast scouting cruisers – to serve a range of tasks, from fleet reconnaissance and the screening of the battle fleet to convoy escort and the use of fast striking forces. This move also reflected a general move in international naval circles from 8in. to 6in. gun cruisers, as they were both cheaper and more versatile than their larger counterparts. In the late 1920s, the Italians felt their most likely adversary would be the French. So, as the Marine Nationale had been building new super-destroyers, the Regia Marina decided to counter them using these *grandi esploratori*. The plans developed by naval architect Giuseppe Vian called for fast, lightly armed cruisers armed with eight 15.2cm guns in four twin turrets. The first these Giussano- (or da Barbiano-) class light cruisers were funded in the 1927–28 budget, and laid down in 1928.

The four Giussanos (*Alberico da Barbiano*, *Alberto da Giussano*, *Bartolomeo Colleoni* and *Giovanni delle Bande Nere)* were far from perfect. Their poor armour offered minimal protection, and so they were vulnerable to the very destroyers they were designed to fight. Their long, narrow hulls made them poor seaboats in rough seas, as they lacked stability. They were also so lightly built that the navy considered them fragile and vulnerable to damage in bad weather, while their crews found them cramped and uncomfortable. Some of these problems were partly overcome before the war, as the hulls were strengthened, but their lack of armour was never remedied. This may have contributed to the fact that all four of them were lost during the war.

The sleek bows of the light cruiser *Alberto da Giussano*, namesake of her class, in dry dock shortly before the war. In 1940 *da Giussano* and her sister ships were some of the fastest cruisers afloat.

Giussano and Cadorna classes (Condottiere type – first and second groups)	
Ships in Giussano class (4): *Alberico da Barbiano, Alberto da Giussano, Bartolomeo Colleoni, Giovanni delle Bande Nere* Ships in Cadorna class (2): *Luigi Cadorna, Armando Diaz*	
In service	1931–33
Displacement	6,844 tons (deep load); Cadornas: 7,001–7,080 tons (deep load)
Dimensions	Length: 169.3m; Beam: 15.5m; Draught: 5.3m

Propulsion	Two shafts, powered by two turbines and six boilers, generating 95,000shp
Maximum speed	36½ knots
Armament	Eight 15.2cm/53 Mod 26 guns in four twin turret (Mod 29 guns in Cadornas), six 10cm/47 AA guns in twin mounts, eight 3.7cm AA guns in twin mounts, eight 13.2mm machine guns in twin mounts, four 53.3cm torpedo tubes in twin mountings
Armour	Main belt: 2.4cm; Deck: 2cm; Turrets: 2.3cm; Conning tower: 2.5–4cm
Sensors	None
Aircraft	Single catapult mounted forward (aft on Cadornas), two Ro43 float planes
Complement	520, Cadornas: 544
Notes	All cruisers designed to carry 111–134 mines, if required.

The 1929–30 budget provided for the building of two more light cruisers. These were essentially repeats of the Giussanos, but they incorporated the hull-strengthening of the earlier ships, and both stability and internal accommodation space were improved. These two cruisers became the Cadorna class, and both *Luigi Cadorna* and *Armando Diaz* entered service in 1933. They carried an improved version of the 15.2cm gun, with a better turret design, and the aircraft catapult was placed amidships rather than in the bow, both of which markedly improved the capabilities of these cruisers. However, they still shared their predecessors' lack of armour. To address the navy's concerns about this lack of protection, the naval architect Umberto Pugliese opted for a more balanced design for the two light cruisers ordered following the 1930–31 budget. The result was a pair of Montecuccoli-class light cruisers (*Raimondo Montecuccoli* and *Muzio Attendolo*).

The Cadorna-class light cruiser *Armando Diaz* took part in the Battle of Calabria (or Punta Stilo) in July 1940, and was then deployed in the Adriatic Sea until early the following year. She was torpedoed and sunk off the Tunisian islands of Kerkennah in late February, while escorting a convoy to Tripoli.

The *Raimondo Montecuccoli*, the namesake of her class, as she appeared shortly before the outbreak of war. As part of the 7th Cruiser Division she took part in the Libyan convoy operation against Force K, and the following summer she saw action in the Battle of Pantelleria.

Montecuccoli class (Condottiere type – third group)

Ships in class (2): *Raimondo Montecuccoli*, *Muzio Attendolo*	
In service	1935
Displacement	8,848–8,853 tons (deep load)
Dimensions	Length: 182.2m; Beam: 16.6m; Draught: 6m
Propulsion	Two shafts, powered by two turbines and six boilers, generating 106,000shp
Maximum speed	37 knots
Armament	Eight 15.2cm/53 Mod 29 guns in four twin turrets, six 10cm /47 AA guns in twin mounts, eight 37mm AA guns in twin mounts, eight 13.2mm machine guns in twin mounts, four 53.3cm torpedo tubes in twin mountings
Armour	Main belt: 6cm; Deck: 2–3cm; Turrets: 7cm; Conning tower: 4–10cm
Sensors	None (*Montecuccoli* fitted with EC-3ter radar in September 1942)
Aircraft	Single catapult mounted amidships, two Ro43 float planes
Complement	650
Notes	All cruisers designed to carry 112–146 mines, if required.

The light cruisers of this third class of Condottieres were notably larger and longer than their predecessors, with a sleeker and more graceful appearance. Their fine lines were helped by modern funnel caps and an elegant clipper bow. Essentially, their protection scheme followed those of the earlier Giussanno and Cadorna classes, but it was over twice as thick and the protected citadel was covered by an armoured deck up to 3cm thick. While the earlier cruisers were vulnerable to fire from the guns mounted on the latest French destroyers, the Montecuccolis offered a degree of protection against fire from enemy cruisers. Their own armament was similar to the earlier Italian light cruisers, but their propulsion systems generated more power, which gave them a marginally higher top speed. Only *Raimondo Montecuccoli* survived the war – *Muzio Attendolo* was sunk in an air attack in December 1942.

The elegant *Emanuele Filiberto Duca d'Aosta*, the namesake of her two-ship class, is pictured in Taranto in early 1941, painted in a rare herringbone camouflage scheme of light olive, painted over a dark grey base. Earlier that year she had formed part of the 8th Division, based in the southern Italian port.

The fourth batch of light cruisers, approved in the 1931–33 budgets, was made up of slightly larger versions of the two Montecuccolis. These became the Duca d'Aosta class, which again consisted of two ships (*Emanuele Filiberto Duca d'Aosta* and *Eugenio di Savoia*). These were 5m longer, to make them more roomy, which in turn led to a rearranged propulsion system. The armoured belt and deck armour were also increased slightly to improve the protection they afforded. These were elegant, fast and well-designed ships, and both of them remained in service until the end of the war. So far, each batch of light cruisers had been larger than the ones before them. Their armament though, had largely remained the same. This was about to change with the fifth batch of Condottiere light cruisers – the two-ship Abruzzi (or Garibaldi) class.

Duca d'Aosta class (Condottiere type – fourth group)

Ships in class (2): *Emanuele Filiberto Duca d'Aosta, Eugenio di Savoia*	
In service	1935–36
Displacement	10,374–10,672 tons (deep load)
Dimensions	Length: 186.9m; Beam: 17.5m; Draught: 6.5m
Propulsion	Two shafts, powered by two turbines and six boilers, generating 110,000shp
Maximum speed	36½ knots
Armament	Eight 15.2cm/53 Mod 29 guns in four twin turrets, six 10cm/47 AA guns in twin mounts, eight 37mm AA guns in twin mounts, twelve 13.2mm machine guns in twin mounts, six 53.3cm torpedo tubes in triple mountings
Armour	Main belt: 7cm; Deck: 3–3.5cm; Turrets: 9cm; Conning tower: 2.5–10cm
Sensors	None (*Duca d'Aosta* fitted with EC-3ter radar in September 1942)
Aircraft	Single catapult mounted amidships, two Ro43 float planes
Complement	694
Notes	Catapults removed in 1943, and twelve 20mm AA guns in twin mounts added

OPPOSITE

In July 1940, *Raimondo Montecuccoli* took part in the Battle of Calabria, and was then used to cover first the Libyan convoys, then the Malta convoys. In June 1942, the cruiser took part in the Battle of Pantelleria. In December 1942, she was damaged in a bombing raid by the USAAF; she remained out of service until just before the armistice.

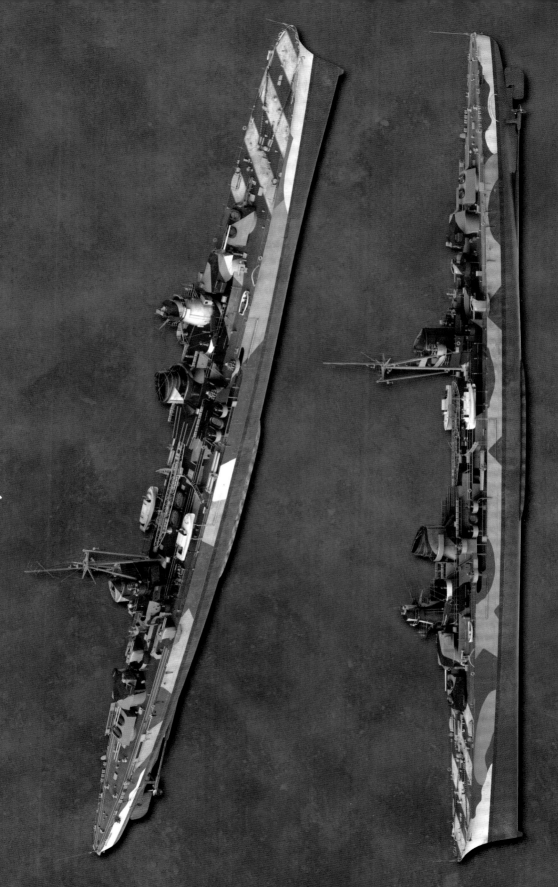

In July 1940 the *Giuseppe Garibaldi*, a Duca degli Abruzzi-class light cruiser, fired the opening salvos of the Battle of Calabria (or Punta Stilo), and damaged the British cruiser *Neptune*. After seeing further action at Matapan the following March, she survived a torpedo hit from a submarine, and went on to operate against the Malta convoys.

Once again, the design of Italian cruisers was influenced by developments in France, where the La Galissoniè class of light cruisers being built was deemed superior to most Italian designs. The *Luigi di Savoia Duca degli Abruzzi* and *Giuseppe Garibaldi* were the Regia Marina's answer to them. Authorized under the 1932–33 programme, they were larger and longer than their predecessors, and much better protected. The Italians had finally accepted the need for larger and better-protected ships, at the expense of speed. The result was an extremely well-balanced cruiser design. The armament increased to ten 15.2cm guns in two twin and two triple turrets, while the protected belt was now 10cm thick, with 3–4cm of deck armour. They still only had two propeller shafts, but they made a very respectable 34 knots. Both Abruzzi-class cruisers survived the war.

Abruzzi class (Condottiere type – fifth group)	
Ships in class (2): *Luigi di Savoia Duca degli Abruzzi, Giuseppe Garibaldi*	
In service	1937
Displacement	11,117–11,575 tons (deep load)
Dimensions	Length: 187m; Beam: 18.9m; Draught: 6.8m
Propulsion	Two shafts, powered by two turbines and eight boilers, generating 100,000shp
Maximum speed	34 knots
Armament	Ten 15.2cm/55 guns Mod 36 in two twin and two triple turrets, eight 10cm/47 AA guns in twin mounts, eight 37mm AA guns in twin mounts, eight 13.2mm machine guns in twin mounts, six 53.3cm (21in.) torpedo tubes in triple mountings
Armour	Main belt: 10cm (3.94in.); Deck: 3–4cm (1.18–1.57in.); Turrets: 13.5cm (5.31in.); Conning tower: 3–10cm (1.18–3.94in.)
Sensors	None
Aircraft	Single catapult mounted amidships, two Ro43 float planes
Complement	692
Notes	All cruisers designed to carry 80–108 mines, if required. During 1942–43, machine guns replaced by ten single 20mm AA guns.

While a sixth version of the Condottieres, the Costanzo class, was planned, based on a slightly modified version of the Abruzzis, this plan was overtaken by the war. With Italy's limited shipyard capacity needed to repair and maintain its existing fleet, these two ships were cancelled before they were laid down. However, in the 1938–39 naval budget, funds were set aside for a class of small light cruisers. These represented a return to the original idea of countering the Marine Nationale's new high-speed super-destroyers. These new Italian cruisers became the twelve-ship Capitani Romani class. These proved themselves capable of making 41 knots, but this was achieved by a complete lack of armour, and a reduction in gun calibre. They mounted eight 13.5cm (5.3in.) guns in four twin turrets. These were all laid down in late 1939, but after the war began production slowed, and four ships were cancelled. In the end, only two of them were actively deployed before the end of the war.

A COMPARISON OF DESIGN AND FUNCTION

Unlike their battleships, the British and Italian cruisers which took an active part in the Mediterranean campaign were all comparatively modern. Moreover, the designs of the Royal Navy and Regia Marina had followed the same basic course. From 1922 until 1930, both navies built what would later be described as heavy cruisers, displacing around 10,000 tons, and armed with 8in. guns. Then, from 1930 until the outbreak of war, the emphasis changed, and smaller light cruisers came in vogue, armed with 6in. guns. There was also some similarity in the rivals' approach to warship design, and the balance between speed, protection and armament. The ships themselves, though, were built with markedly different roles in mind.

In terms of heavy cruisers, the British vessels were designed as ocean cruisers, where good endurance and seakeeping qualities were major design considerations. Protection was less important. At first, the Italian emphasis was on speed rather than protection. Strangely, both nations produced vessels with broadly similar offensive capabilities. This, of course, wasn't surprising, as for the most part they mounted the same number and calibre of guns. Both navies also used broadly similar fire direction systems, although by 1941 the Royal Navy's superiority in radar had given it a distinct advantage, especially at night. Another British advantage in a prolonged fight was that its heavy cruisers were more resilient to absorbing damage. This was less due to armoured protection than a combination of less tangible factors, such as the robustness of propulsion systems, ship stability, damage control provision and effective watertight integrity.

The two navies also envisaged different roles for their cruisers. The cruisers of the Regia Marina were designed to form part of a balanced battle fleet, serving either as a screen protecting the battleships, or as a foil to thwart attacks by enemy cruisers or destroyers. Italian light cruisers were also developed to act in a scouting capacity,

At the Battle of Cape Spada on 19 July 1940, the shortcomings of Italian light cruiser designs were exposed. There, the armour of the da Giussano-class light cruiser *Bartolomeo Colleoni* was too thin to protect her from the fire of enemy destroyers, let alone the 6in. shells that immobilized her.

The Abruzzi class was the last two of Italy's Condottiere batch of light cruisers, and entered service in 1937. The design of the ships was well-balanced, with greater firepower and better protection than previous Italian light cruisers, while still retaining a reasonable top speed. The *Luigi di Savoia Duca degli Abruzzi* is shown here shortly before the outbreak of the war.

augmented, of course, by land-based aircraft and the fleet's own scouting aircraft. For the British, due to their designed role, there was no real place for heavy cruisers in the battle fleet. Instead, the job of fleet protection fell to light cruisers and destroyers, augmented by torpedo-carrying carrier planes. As a result, relatively few heavy cruisers were deployed in the Mediterranean Fleet.

Originally, Italian light cruisers were designed as scouting cruisers, to counter the powerful destroyers then being built by the French. During the war, they were employed in a variety of roles, including fleet and convoy protection, and in the formation of naval striking groups. The British, though, built their first classes of light cruisers with a view to performing the same duties, but also demanded the Leanders perform a trade protection role. The Arethusas which followed them, and all subsequent British light cruisers, were primarily designed to fulfil a fleet protection role. Given the limited speed of most capital ships in the Royal Navy, the design emphasis was on firepower rather than speed. The Southamptons and Fijis were the ideal cruisers for this task.

One advantage the Italians cruisers enjoyed was their superior speed. Cautious rules of engagement limited the effectiveness of the Italian battle fleet in 1940–41. So, this edge in speed was often used to avoid contact rather than to initiate it. Freed of these operational restraints, as the Italian cruisers were during the convoy battles off Pantelleria in 1942, this advantage in speed could be put to good use in launching sudden strikes against the Malta convoys. The British and Commonwealth navies did the same, as Force K operated in this manner against Italian convoys off the Libyan coast. These cruisers were not as well designed for this striking role as their Italian counterparts.

The cruisers of the Regia Marina can be likened to sleek, fast thoroughbreds, but forced to run a race for which they were not ideally suited. They were designed for speed, and for the most part lacked the armour needed to fight lengthy engagements. Until the coming of the Southampton class, the cruisers of the two navies enjoyed a relative parity in terms of firepower. However, these new cruisers meant that the Royal Navy enjoyed a comparative edge over their lightly protected Italian counterparts. The Italians only achieved a balance between firepower, protection and speed with the Zaras and Abruzzis. If Italian naval architects had got over their preoccupation with speed sooner, then the Regia Marina's cruiser fleet might well have given a much better account of itself. The British, with their more balanced approach to cruiser design, were better placed to last the pace.

THE STRATEGIC SITUATION

By June 1940, the war in Europe was ten months old. Since 3 September 1939 the Royal Navy had been fully committed to the war against Nazi Germany, and while this period was described as 'The Phoney War', this never applied at sea. There had been successes and losses on both sides, the most notable being the sinking of the British battleship *Royal Oak* in Scapa Flow in October 1939, and the loss of the German armoured cruiser *Admiral Graf Spee* two months later. During this time, the British Mediterranean Fleet had been sidelined, as British and German naval efforts were concentrated on the Atlantic theatre. The Phoney War came to an abrupt end in April 1940, when the Germans invaded Denmark and Norway. The Royal Navy was heavily committed to the Norwegian campaign, and both sides suffered significant losses. However, these events were quickly overshadowed on 10 May, when the Germans invaded France and the Low Countries.

The German blitzkrieg was spectacularly successful, and British, Belgian and French forces were quickly pushed back towards the Channel ports. By late May, the Royal Navy was called upon to help evacuate the thousands of Allied troops trapped around Dunkirk. This it did, helped by civilian craft, and despite heavy British losses, over a third of a million Allied troops were rescued. The evacuation was completed on 4 June, by which time the Germans were driving on Paris. In Rome, the Italian leader Benito Mussolini realized that if he remained neutral then Italy would be unable to reap any dividend from the fall of France. So, on 10 June 1940, four days before the fall of Paris, Italy formally declared war, both on France and her allies. The following day the Italians bombed Malta for the first time. Malta had traditionally been the base of Britain's Mediterranean Fleet. As the risk of war with Italy increased, the fleet was moved to Alexandria in Egypt, beyond the reach of Italian bombers. So, Britain held both ends of the Mediterranean, while Italy held its centre.

Until then, the French Marine Nationale had been the dominant force in the Western Mediterranean. After the fall of France, the French Mediterranean Fleet was controlled by Vichy France, a German ally. This posed an unacceptable risk to the British, and so it was decided to neutralize the French fleet, either willingly or by force. While the French squadron in Alexandria acceded, the admiral commanding the bulk of the French fleet refused to negotiate. So, on 3 July, British warships bombarded the French fleet at Mers-el-Kébir in French Algeria, sinking a battleship and damaging two more. Despite the trauma this caused, the neutralization of the French fleet was the only course left open to Britain. Consequently, the British Mediterranean Fleet stood alone against the Regia Marina.

The Mediterranean Fleet was commanded by the highly experienced Admiral Sir Andrew Cunningham, who usually operated from his flagship *Warspite*. For him, the complex naval situation he faced boiled down to one thing. Historically, the fleet existed to keep open Britain's sea route to India and the Far East, by way of the Suez Canal. The Regia Marina was blocking this strategically vital maritime line of communication. So, if it could be reopened, this would avoid British ships making the much longer voyage around Africa by way of the Cape of Good Hope. That, though, meant contesting the Italian naval dominance in the Central Mediterranean. His secondary objective was to establish sea control over the waters of the Eastern Mediterranean, in order to protect British interests there. Then, by attacking the sea lanes to its Libyan colony in North Africa, Cunningham would be able to relieve pressure on the British army charged with defending Egypt.

The neutralization of the French fleet meant that there was a strategic naval void in the Western Mediterranean. In late June, the Admiralty decided to fill this by building up its forces based in Gibraltar. So, Force H was established there, under the command of the highly competent Vice Admiral Sir James Somerville. It was initially built around the battlecruiser *Hood* and the aircraft carrier *Ark Royal*, and was first blooded at Mers-el-Kébir. Over the course of the war, its strength fluctuated

The action off Cape Spada on 19 July 1940 witnessed the end of *Bartolomeo Colleoni*. At 0841hrs the *Bartolomeo Colleoni* was hit by a torpedo fired by the destroyer *Ilex*, which blew off the cruiser's bow. A minute later she was hit amidships by another 21in. torpedo fired by *Hyperion*. This shows the Italian cruiser at the moment this second torpedo struck.

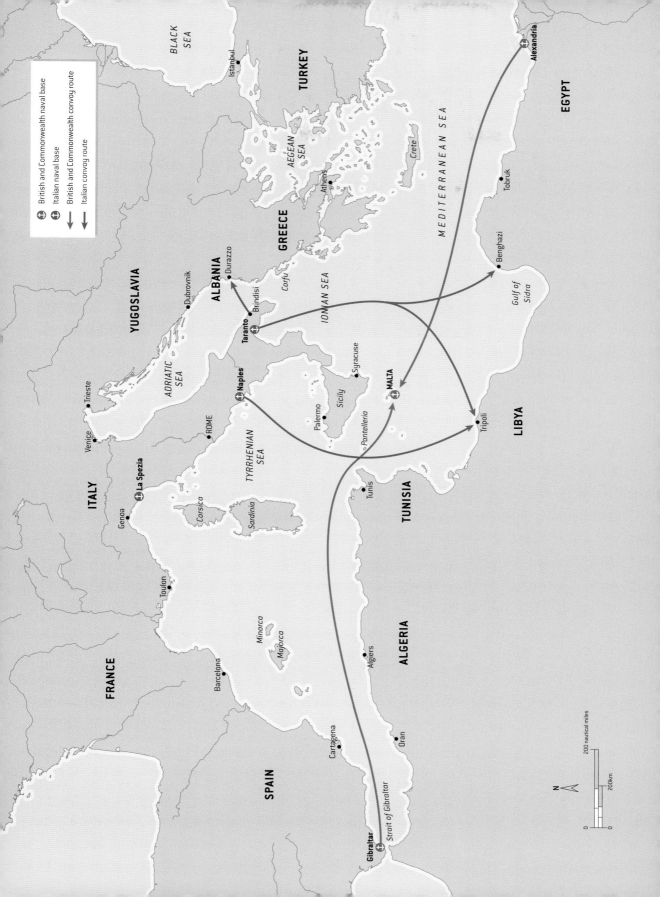

BLACK
SEA

TURKEY

Istanbul

British and Commonwealth naval base
Italian naval base
British and Commonwealth convoy route
Italian convoy route

AEGEAN
SEA

GREECE

Athens

Crete

MEDITERRANEAN SEA

EGYPT

Alexandria

Tobruk

Benghazi

YUGOSLAVIA

Dubrovnik

ALBANIA

Durazzo

Corfu

Brindisi

IONIAN SEA

Gulf of
Sidra

Taranto

ADRIATIC
SEA

Trieste

Venice

Naples

Syracuse

MALTA

LIBYA

Tripoli

ITALY

ROME

Palermo

Sicily

Pantelleria

La Spezia

TYRRHENIAN
SEA

Genoa

Corsica

Sardinia

Tunis

TUNISIA

Toulon

Minorca

Majorca

Algiers

ALGERIA

FRANCE

Barcelona

Cartagena

Oran

SPAIN

Gibraltar

Strait of Gibraltar

N

200 nautical miles

200km

The four Zara-class heavy cruisers of Rear Admiral Mattecucci's 1st Cruiser Division, pictured berthed in Naples during late 1940. That November, three of them – the division flagship *Pola* and her sister ships *Fiume* and *Gorizia* would take part in the Battle of Spartivento.

in line with its ever-changing operational requirements. Officially, Force H was nominally under the command of the Flag Officer North Atlantic who was also based in Gibraltar, but in practice Somerville answered directly to the Admiralty in London. In effect, Force H was there to establish and maintain a British naval presence in the Western Mediterranean. However, it could also be called upon to venture into the Atlantic, as it did with dramatic success during the hunt for the *Bismarck* in May 1941.

Increasingly though, Somerville's job was to protect convoys bound for Malta. This strategically important fortress island became the junction between Cunningham's command in the east and Somerville's in the west. During these often complex operations in the Mediterranean, overall control was exercised by Admiral Cunningham. By 1941, as the convoy battles for Malta intensified, a small force of cruisers and destroyers was temporarily stationed in Malta. Both it and the submarine flotilla based there were used to attack Italian sea routes to Libya, which passed close to the beleaguered island. These proved a major thorn in the Regia Marina's side. If the survivors of any convoys which reached Malta were to continue to Egypt, or west-bound convoys had to be handed over to Somerville's protection, then the Mediterranean Fleet would escort them to and from Maltese waters. However, this brought Cunningham's battle fleet within striking range of the Regia Marina.

This, though, was part of Cunningham's plan. He wanted to bring the Italians to battle, in order to reduce the potency of their battle fleet. Its effectiveness was markedly reduced in November 1940, when the Fleet Air Arm carried out a daring air attack on the Italian fleet's base at Taranto. From that point on Cunningham held the initiative in the waters to the east of Malta, although more dramatic clashes would take place, including the Battle of Matapan in March 1941. By then, the British and their Commonwealth allies had become deeply embroiled in Greece, a campaign which ended in disaster, following German intervention in the region. This, followed by the

equally disastrous battle for Crete, saw the Royal Navy forced to evacuate Allied troops in the face of overwhelming German air superiority. The Mediterranean Fleet suffered heavy losses in the campaign, but Cunningham was determined to continue his aggressive strategy, which saw him gradually re-establish naval control of the Eastern Mediterranean.

By late 1942, after the Second Battle of El Alamein and the Allied landings in Morocco and Algeria, the strategic situation in North Africa began to change rapidly. After the fall of Tripoli on 23 January 1943, the remaining Axis forces in Libya withdrew into Tunisia. The campaign there lasted until May 1943, but with

The Leander-class light cruiser *Ajax*, pictured on 6 April 1941 at the docks at Piraeus near Athens, unloading British and Commonwealth troops sent to support the Greek Army. Within weeks the surviving troops were being evacuated, first to Crete, and then back to Egypt. It was *Ajax* that evacuated the last of these troops from the same quayside on 29 April.

In this panorama of Suda Bay in north-western Crete, taken in mid-May 1941, the anchorage is shown covered by the smoke of burning transport ships. In the centre lies the heavy cruiser *York*, which, on 26 March, was crippled in an attack by Italian torpedo-armed motor boats. *York* was blown up and abandoned there on 22 May.

The light cruiser *Giovanni delle Bande Nere*, pictured before the outbreak of war. On 19 July 1940, as the flagship of Rear Admiral Casardi's small 2nd Division, she was damaged in the Battle of Cape Spada, when her sister ship *Bartolomeo Colleoni* was sunk. She survived the action, but would fall victim to British destroyers off Cape Bon five months later.

Allied armies attacking the Axis from both east and west, the result was hardly in doubt. These Allied successes on land meant that the crisis facing Malta began to ease. That in turn paved the way for subsequent Allied landings in Sicily in July, and landings in southern Italy in September. The Mediterranean Fleet was increasingly based in freshly captured North African ports, and would eventually be based at Algiers. It would also be divided into a number of regional commands. However, in October 1943, after the Italian armistice, Cunningham was promoted to First Sea Lord, and his command was handed over to his unrelated namesake, Admiral Sir John Cunningham.

The problems of Cunningham's Italian counterparts were both similar and uniquely different. In late May 1940, just days before Italy entered the war, the Supermarina – the Italian equivalent of the Admiralty – issued its war plan. It saw the Central Mediterranean as its key battleground. The Regia Marina would protect Italian convoy routes to Libya and Albania, and blockade the straits between Sicily and Tunisia, which would sever the British sea route through the Mediterranean. The Italian Air Force would support this blockade, and would attack any enemy forces entering the Central Mediterranean. Only light forces and submarines would range further east and west. Instead, the battle fleet would be held back within this central area, and deployed only after the British fleet was worn down by air and submarine attacks. In other words, the battle fleet would only engage the British close to friendly bases such as Taranto and Naples, and only when tactical and numerical conditions were favourable.

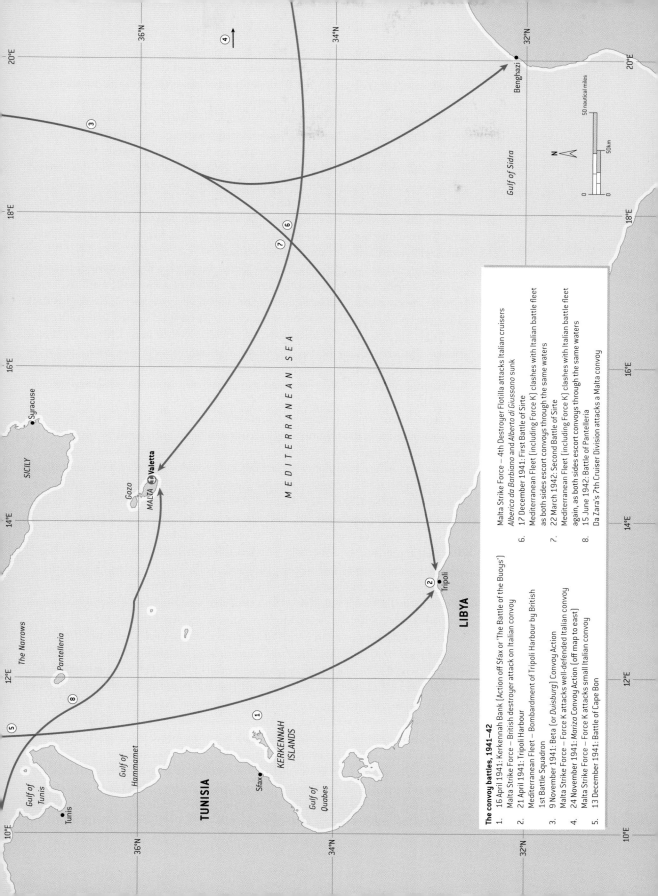

The convoy battles, 1941–42

1. 16 April 1941: Kerkennah Bank (Action off Sfax or 'The Battle of the Buoys')
   Malta Strike Force – British destroyer attack on Italian convoy
2. 21 April 1941: Tripoli Harbour
   Mediterranean Fleet – Bombardment of Tripoli Harbour by British
   1st Battle Squadron
3. 9 November 1941: Beta (or *Duisburg*) Convoy Action
   Malta Strike Force – Force K attacks well-defended Italian convoy
4. 24 November 1941: *Mariza* Convoy Action [off map to east]
   Malta Strike Force – Force K attacks small Italian convoy
5. 13 December 1941: Battle of Cape Bon
   Malta Strike Force – Force K attacks a Malta convoy
6. Malta Strike Force – 4th Destroyer Flotilla attacks Italian cruisers
   Alberico da Barbiano and *Alberto di Giussano* sunk
7. 17 December 1941: First Battle of Sirte
   Mediterranean Fleet (including Force K) clashes with Italian battle fleet
   as both sides escort convoys through the same waters
8. 22 March 1942: Second Battle of Sirte
   Mediterranean Fleet (including Force K) clashes with Italian battle fleet
   again, as both sides escort convoys through the same waters
   15 June 1942: Battle of Pantelleria
   Da Zara's 7th Cruiser Division attacks a Malta convoy

In general, this somewhat restrained plan was followed throughout the campaign. It made sense, as it played to Italy's strengths – her powerful air force, the ability to easily concentrate the battle fleet, the proximity to her own air and naval bases and the central position Italy held in the Mediterranean. When the Regia Marina ventured out of this central area, and into the Eastern Mediterranean, the operation ended in disaster, with three of the fleet's heavy cruisers being lost. However, this largely defensive plan was mitigated by other factors. First, despite the near parity of forces, there was clearly a need to bring Cunningham's fleet to battle before it could be reinforced. For much of the war, the battle fleet was frequently deployed to support convoys sailing between Italy and Libya. This protection became even more necessary after British cruisers and destroyers began operating from Malta. By then the island itself had become a major strategic focal point.

During 1941–42 the Regia Marina was drawn into a series of punishing operations against the Malta convoys. While Axis aircraft and submarines were the main assailants in these convoy attacks, the surface arm of the Italian navy was also involved, after the Supermarina approved the creation of fast cruiser-based striking forces, which would use strike and run tactics to wear down the convoys as they neared Malta. By then, though, the strength of the navy had been depleted through war losses, and fuel shortages were beginning to make themselves felt. So, during this crucial period, these lighter units of the battle fleet were used more frequently, while the battleships tended to remain in port.

During the campaign, Admiral Cunningham enjoyed a considerable degree of freedom in terms of the planning and execution of naval operations. By contrast, the Regia Marina suffered from a complex command structure, which tended to inhibit initiative and reduced the ability to react quickly to events. In theory, naval operations were controlled by Ammiraglio d'Armata (Admiral) Domenico Cavagnari, assisted by Ammiraglio di Squadra (Vice Admiral) Odoardo Somigli. In late 1940, in the aftermath of the Taranto debacle, they were replaced by vice admirals Arturo Ricardi and Inigo Campioni respectively. This in turn led to a drive to make the command structure more flexible, especially between the Supermarina and the battle fleet. However, initiative was still discouraged, and the Regia Marina was plagued by a heavily centralized command structure for the duration of the war.

The battle fleet itself was divided into two large squadrons (which were more akin to small fleets), with the fleet's modern cruisers divided between the two. Italy's battleships were concentrated in the 1st Squadron, which, until December 1940, was commanded by Campioni. The 2nd Squadron was commanded by Vice Admiral Paladini, who flew his flag in the heavy cruiser *Pola*. In December, these two squadrons were amalgamated, and remained so until January 1942, when the two-squadron structure was reintroduced, albeit under a new Naval Forces command. By then, though, the tendency was to use smaller formations, such as ad hoc *gruppi* ('groups') or detached squadrons for specific duties, such as convoy protection, or the interception of enemy forces. While this evolving command structure may have been problematic, the Regia Marina benefited from a clarity of purpose, as it never strayed far from its initial war plans. As a result, despite mounting losses, the Italian navy largely succeeded in achieving its aims, until it was eventually overtaken by political and military events beyond its control.

TECHNICAL
SPECIFICATIONS

FIREPOWER

Generally, the 6in. and 8in. guns mounted in British and Italian cruisers were similar in terms of reliability and performance. The British 8in./50 Mark VIII gun was specifically designed for Britain's treaty cruisers, and entered service in 1927, when the Kents were being fitted out. It fired a 256lb semi-armour-piercing common (SAPC) or high explosive (HE) projectile, with a maximum range of 29,000 yards – 15½ sea miles in gunnery terms – the equivalent of just over 14 nautical miles. In normal circumstances, the shell could be expected to penetrate the armour of an enemy heavy cruiser at around half that range. Its rate of fire was approximately four rounds a minute.

The Ansaldo 20.3cm/50 Model 24 gun mounted in the Italian Trentos fired a 125.3kg armour-piercing (AP) shell up to 28,000m, but the gun had a slower rate of fire of up to three rounds a minute, although this reduced to one round when the gun was elevated to fire at maximum range. The marginally more powerful Ansaldo 20.3cm/53 Model 27 or Model 29 gun mounted in *Bolzano* and the Zaras fired the same shell. The only difference in the barrels was that the Model 29 in *Bolzano* had lighter mountings. These guns had a theoretical maximum range of 31,566m. The effective range, though, was less than 27,000m, and to penetrate the armour of a

The Italian Cadorna-class light cruiser *Bartolomeo Colleoni* under attack from the Australian cruiser *Sydney* and destroyers of the 2nd Flotilla, at the Battle of Cape Spada on the morning of 19 July 1940. At 0825hrs she was disabled by a shell from *Sydney*, as she tried to escape.

typical British heavy cruiser this was reduced further to 15,000m. Its rate of fire was slightly improved, at three to four rounds per minute.

From the Leanders on, all British and Commonwealth light cruisers mounted the 6in./50 BL Mark XXIII gun, which first entered service in 1933 when *Leander* was being fitted out in Portsmouth. The gun fired a 112lb common pointed ballistic cap (CPBC) shell, which was a semi-armour-piercing round, or an HE round for shore bombardment missions. It had a range of up to 24,500 yards, but effective range was half that. Normal rate of fire was around six rounds a minute. However, as these guns were hand-loaded after the shell and charge reached the turret, a higher rate of fire of around eight rounds a minute was possible for short periods, until the crew were worn out by the extra labour. In theory, as the hoists could supply ten rounds a minute, in extremis this could be increased.

The Italian 15.2cm/53 gun was carried in all Condottiere-type light cruisers, apart from the Abruzzi class. The Model 1926 and Model 1929 guns were identical, but the older model fitted in the Giussanos was manufactured by Ansaldo, while the others were made by OTO, and mounted in the next three classes. The guns entered service in 1928 and 1930 respectively. They fired an AP round weighing 47.5kg, although an HE round was also carried. Its maximum range was listed as 22,600m, and its rate of fire was approximately five rounds per minute. Like the larger Italian guns, electrical power was used for all loading procedures, including operating the chain rammer. The 15.2cm/55 gun Model 1934 mounted in the Abruzzis fired a slightly heavier 50kg AP shell, and had a maximum range of 25,740m. It managed a rate of fire of five to six rounds per minute.

The British guns were reliable and accurate, and by 1940, initial hydraulic problems with the 8in. gun turrets had been overcome. Their only weakness was the lack

This hurriedly taken action shot is one of a short sequence, photographed from the bridge of the Dido-class cruiser *Euryalus* on 22 March 1942, during the Second Battle of Sirte as she engages the Italian fleet. Ahead of her, Vian's flagship *Cleopatra* can be seen laying a smoke screen.

BRITISH LIGHT CRUISER GUN TURRET

The 6in./50 BL gun Mark XXIII was mounted in all British and Commonwealth light cruisers built from 1930 onwards. First introduced in 1933, it was a reliable, accurate weapon, but compared to similar ordnance used by other navies it appeared slightly old fashioned. This was because unlike most of its foreign contemporaries, although shells were hoisted to the turret mechanically using an 'endless chain', the gun still relied on manual ramming and manual operation of its breech mechanism. This though, had its advantages. In theory the weapon had an average rate of fire of six rounds a minute. The chain-style ammunition hoist could bring it up to

16 rounds a minute. So, in action, for several crucial minutes until the crew tired, this rate of fire could be increased. This gave the more archaic British system a temporarily higher rate of fire than its more sophisticated Italian counterpart. This diagram shows the three-gun Mark XXIII mounting used in the Fiji and Edinburgh classes. However, its general layout and operation was similar to the two-gun Mark XXI turret mountings in the Leanders and Arethusas, and the three-gun Mark XXII mounting in the Southamptons. A surviving example of this turret can be found on the historic ship HMS *Belfast*.

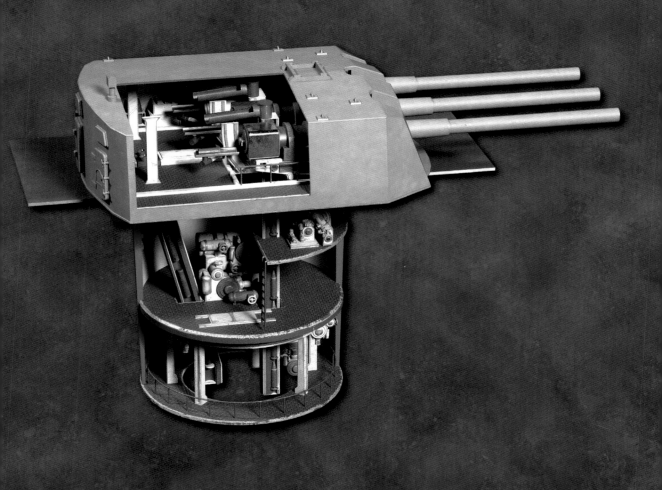

The light cruiser *Gorizia*, pictured firing her main battery at British light cruisers during the Second Battle of Sirte, on 22 March 1942. *Gorizia*, *Trento* and *Bande Nere* formed Rear Admiral Parona's Gruppa Gorizia during this operation.

of protection for these heavy cruiser turrets, which meant the guns and crew were particularly vulnerable to even light splinter damage. The 6in. guns of the light cruisers were equally reliable, having been developed from ordnance used during World War I. The Mark XXIII was essentially a modernized version of these older weapons. It had originally been intended that these would have an anti-aircraft capability, but this proved impractical. As noted above, these manually loaded guns could be operated at an increased rate for short periods, but only at ranges of less than 10,000 yards, as beyond that the higher elevation of the guns made this rapid loading impossible.

These guns worked perfectly in twin gun turrets. However, the introduction of the triple gun turret in the Southamptons created a problem, as shells fired by the centre barrel would have their flight disrupted by the blast from the outer barrels, which reduced accuracy. By 1940, though, this problem had been solved by setting the central barrel back slightly inside the turret, and delaying this gun's fire by a second. The Italians also suffered accuracy problems, but these were less easily dealt with. It was found that salvos fired by Italian heavy and light cruisers rarely landed in a tight grouping. This reduced the chances of scoring one or more hits on a target. On examination, it was found that this dispersal of the salvo was caused by the way the guns were mounted. In Italian cruisers, the two barrels in a turret were mounted on a single cradle. The result was that the guns were too close together, and so when fired, the blast would deflect the shells slightly.

Essentially, it was a similar problem to that which was encountered by the British with their triple turrets. In the case of the Regia Marina, though, this was exacerbated by the higher muzzle velocity of the Italian guns, and inconsistencies in the

In this photograph taken from the bridge of *Euryalus* during the Second Battle of Sirte, Vian's flagship *Cleopatra* has now laid a thick black smoke screen from her funnels, while *Euryalus* and *Dido* astern of her have done the same.

ITALIAN LIGHT CRUISER GUN TURRET

All but the last batch of Condottiere-type light cruisers mounted the same type of 15.2cm/53 gun. The Cadornas mounted a Model 1926 gun, produced by Ansaldo, while the others carried the Model 1929, manufactured by OTO. The turret shown here mounts the OTO guns. There were minor differences between the two models, which meant that parts weren't usually interchangeable. They worked slightly differently too. In the Cadornas, a mechanical loader transferred the shell from the hoist to the breech, and stayed there while a mechanical rammer slid the shell into the breech. In the slightly more complex OTO version, a reciprocating lever swung the shell into a loading tray, then the rammer did the rest, while the lever slid down to pick up the next shell. It was a faster system than the Ansaldo version, and could fire six rounds a minute, compared to the four rounds of the older system. However, it was more complex, and therefore harder to maintain.

These turrets used electrical power to operate all aspects of the loading system, including the extraction of the spent shell cases. One major drawback of the system was that the two guns in the turret shared the same cradle. That meant they were close to each other, the barrels just 75cm apart. As a result, when the guns were fired, the blast forced the shell slightly off its intended path, which led to the dispersal of the cruiser's fall of shot.

performance of their powder charges. In action, British observers noted that while gunnery from Italian cruisers was accurately ranged on their targets, the widely dispersed fall of shot made the Italian salvo considerably less effective than it should have been. In theory, the problem should have been solved with the introduction of the slightly lower-velocity Model 1934 guns mounted in the Abruzzis. There, though, the Italians encountered the same problem as the British – the shell fired from the central barrel of a triple turret was prone to being deflected. However, the Italians never managed to design an adequate solution to this problem.

While most British and Italian cruisers carried torpedoes, these had fairly limited combat value, as large-scale torpedo attacks were more the preserve of destroyer flotillas than cruisers. They were more likely to be used to finish off stricken warships of either side, or to force enemy attackers to turn away from a torpedo spread than as a viable offensive weapon. In any case, both fleets used torpedoes of the same size – 21in. The British Mark IX torpedo carried 805lb of Torpex, and had a range of 11,000 yards at 41 knots. Its Italian counterpart the Silurificio 270 M would run for 8,750 yards at 35 knots, and carried a 270kg warhead.

At the start of the war, the cruisers of both navies were relatively poorly protected against air attack. The British relied on their secondary battery directed by the ship's HACS system to lay down a curtain of flak in the path of enemy bombers, and in this the 4in. Mark XVI QF gun proved reasonably effective. This reliability increased as Type 285 AA fire control radar became available in 1942–43. Closer defence was provided by multiple 2pdr pom-poms and 0.5in. machine guns. These proved less effective, and as the war went on they were gradually replaced by 40mm Bofors and 20mm Oerlikon guns. In Italian cruisers, the medium calibre OTO 10cm/47 AA gun fulfilled a similar role to its British counterpart, laying down a flak barrage. It wasn't suitable for accurate, aimed fire. More effective was the Breda 37mm/54 AA gun, which performed similarly to its British counterpart, the 2pdr. The 13.2mm machine gun was also used, but where possible these were replaced by singly mounted Breda 20mm/70 light AA guns, first developed in 1939.

The 5.25in. QF Mark I mounted in the Dido class had a much better performance, and could fire seven rounds a minute, with an AA ceiling of 46,500ft. So, it was a highly effective barrage weapon, but linked to the Type 285 radar it became a very effective anti-aircraft weapon. It could also be used against surface targets. With a maximum range of 25,070 yards, its semi-armour-piercing shells could penetrate 3in. of armour at 9,500 yards. This, coupled with its impressive rate of fire and radar fire control, made it an extremely useful surface weapon at close range.

GUNNERY DIRECTION

During World War II, a warship's guns were only as effective as the system used to direct their fire. Gunnery direction (or fire control) systems were developed before World War I as a way to coordinate all the fire of a warship's main guns. Optical rangefinders were used to calculate the range and bearing of a target. This, together with data on the course and speed of target and firer, were fed into a mechanical

A reproduction of a painting by Lieutenant-Commander Rowland Langmaid depicting Rear Admiral Glennie's Force D in action against an Axis invasion force off Cape Spada, on the night of 21–22 May 1941. As Glennie's flagship *Dido*, followed by *Orion* and *Ajax*, illuminate the little Greek fishing vessels used as troop transports, they and the destroyers then sweep them with point-blank fire.

computing machine, along with other factors such as wind, temperature and humidity. The machine would then calculate a firing solution, which was passed on to the ship's gunnery officer, and from him to the turrets. Each gun would be given its required elevation and bearing. When all turrets were ready, the gunnery officer would fire a salvo. Spotters would watch where the shell splashes landed, and salvos were then corrected until the shells straddled (landed around) the target. In both British and Italian cruisers, the gunnery officer sat in a director control tower (DCT), sited on top of the cruiser's superstructure.

The computing machine, known in the Royal Navy as an Admiralty Fire Control Table (AFCT), was located in a plotting room inside the ship's hull. In British cruisers, a plotting officer supervised the plotting room team (which ensured there was a steady flow of firing solutions for the gunnery officer) and the turrets, and made sure that information was fed to the DCT and the turrets. The Regia Marina relied on the British-designed Barr and Stroud fire control table, produced under licence in Italy. This was a reliable and effective analogue gunnery computer, similar to the ones used in British cruisers, albeit in a slightly simpler and older form.

The British cruisers used 15ft-long Barr and Stroud coincidence rangefinders, mounted in the DCTs, which operated by superimposing one image of the target on another. When the images lined up, the range was read off a calibrated scale. Like their British counterparts, most Italian cruisers had two fire-control directors, one forward, the other aft. These were fitted with 5m-long Galileo coincidence rangefinders, and 3m or 5m stereoscopic scartometers, which measured the deviation of the salvo. From the Montecuccolis on, a single fire control director was emplaced on top of the bridge superstructure, mounting a stabilized 7.2m-long

The forward 6in. guns of the Giussano-class light cruiser *Alberico da Barbiano*. While these guns were reliable pieces of ordnance, they were let down by their mounting, as the close proximity of the barrels caused distortion to the flight path of the shells, which resulted in salvo dispersion.

Galileo rangefinder, which combined both functions. In the heavy cruiser, the secondary battery was directed by its own dedicated 3m-long Galileo rangefinder.

During this period radar was in its infancy, but increasingly reliable sets were developed as the campaign wore on. In most wartime cruisers, radar sets were mounted in the masts or atop the superstructure, to provide the best possible range and coverage. Essentially, radar came in two forms. Surface search or air search radar was used to detect an enemy ship or aircraft. While surface detection ranges were initially quite short, radar gave cruisers a better chance to detect the enemy at night. In June 1940 only a handful of British cruisers carried radar, and this was usually a primitive Type 79Y air search set. However, during that year Type 281 air search sets were installed, together with the more useful Type 279, which was dual purpose (air and surface), and could detect surface contacts at 23 nautical miles. Type 273, a more accurate surface search radar, was introduced in 1941, with a range of 19 miles. Most of these sets resembled modern hospital monitors. However, by 1943, modern plan position indicator (PPI) displays were developed, with the ship at the centre of the screen.

The second type was fire control radar, used to gather information which could be fed into the ship's computer plotter, and used to create fire control solutions, even when the target couldn't be seen visually. From late 1940, Type 284 fire control radars began to be fitted in British cruisers, giving them the ability to conduct accurate radar-guided gunnery. Various improved versions of this set followed as the war progressed. Type 285 was a similar system, but designed for anti-aircraft guns. Generally, as these radar sets were installed in cruisers during 1940–41, the Royal Navy began enjoying a significant edge over its Italian opponents. While search radar usually didn't exceed visual detection ranges in daylight, these sets gave the British a significant advantage during night operations. This, combined with increasingly sophisticated fire control sets, gave the Royal Navy an immense qualitative edge over its Italian foes.

Italian cruisers lacked radar throughout the first crucial years of the war. It was only in mid-1943 that the EC3ter *Gufo* (Owl) radar system was introduced, and only a few of these were fitted before the armistice. The only cruiser to benefit from it was the *Eugenio di Savoia*. The *Gufo* was primitive compared to contemporary Allied radars; its surface detection range of 16 nautical miles made it useful in night actions, although it wasn't accurate enough to be used in a radar fire control capacity. It also functioned as an air search radar. In August 1943, just before the armistice and therefore too late to be used operationally, the *Abruzzi* was fitted with a German FuMo 24 radar, which had a surface detection range of 11 miles, but which also functioned as a fire control radar. So, throughout the campaign, this lack of radar meant that the Regia Marina's cruisers were placed at a critical operational disadvantage.

PROTECTION

In the majority of cruisers designed and built during the interwar period, protection was considered less important than speed and firepower. Designers found that to keep within the 10,000-ton standard tonnage ceiling while still mounting eight 8in. guns, little weight was left for armour. So to save weight, the British County-type heavy

FIRE CONTROL SYSTEM, BRITISH LIGHT CRUISER, 1941–42

By 1940 most of the world's major navies had developed similar fire control systems for their larger guns. Those used in the cruisers of the Royal Navy and the Regia Marina were remarkably similar, save for the quality and size of rangefinders, and minor differences in the analogue fire control computers used. The only major difference occurred as the war progressed, as fire control radar systems were fitted in British cruisers. This diagram shows the gunnery direction system in the British Arethusa-class light cruiser *Penelope* in late 1942.

Information gathered from visual rangefinders or the ship's main fire control radar was fed to the Fire Control Table located in the Plotting Room. This was then processed, and a fire control solution produced. This was then passed to the gunnery officer in the main gunnery director, and then transmitted to each of the gun turrets in the form of elevation and bearing. Once all of the ship's main guns were ready to fire, the gunnery officer would then issue the order to shoot. Once the salvo landed, a spotting team in the main gunnery director would note where it landed, and feed this information back into the Fire Control Table, which would then update the firing solution, to improve the accuracy of the next salvo.

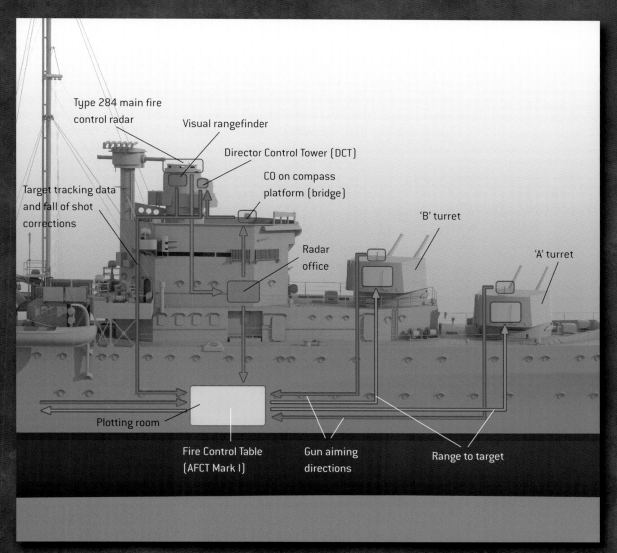

Type 284 main fire control radar

Visual rangefinder

Director Control Tower (DCT)

CO on compass platform (bridge)

Target tracking data and fall of shot corrections

Radar office

'B' turret

'A' turret

Plotting room

Fire Control Table (AFCT Mark I)

Gun aiming directions

Range to target

In the action off Cape Spada on 19 July 1940, the *Bartolomeo Colleoni* was immobilized by fire from the Australian light cruiser *Sydney*. She was then finished off by torpedoes launched at point-blank range by the destroyer *Hyperion*. She capsized and sank within minutes.

cruisers were protected by a thin box of armour around their turrets, machinery spaces and magazines. Italy's Trento class used a similar box system, but in places this was even thinner than in the British Kents. The result was a cruiser described by its detractors as 'eggshells armed with hammers'. Italian naval officers similarly described the Trentos as 'glass ships with big guns'. This was one of the reasons the Royal Navy rarely deployed its heavy cruisers in Mediterranean waters. After all, these ships were designed for the more global role of trade protection. The Italians, though, realized the shortcoming of the Trentos, and adopted a more balanced approach for the Zara class.

The same lack of protection was repeated in the first of the Condottiere group of Italian light cruisers. This deficiency was partly addressed in the Montecuccoli and Duca d'Aosta classes, but it was not until the arrival of the Abruzzis that a more effective balance was found. British light cruisers went through a similar but less dramatic development, with the box protection system meaning that while magazines and propulsion spaces were adequately protected, the rest of the ship was not. A CPBC shell fired by a British 6in./50 Mark XXIII gun could penetrate 3in. of armour at 12,500 yards, while plunging fire at 22,000 yards could penetrate 2in. of deck armour. That was enough to penetrate the hull of all Italian cruisers, apart from the Zaras and Abruzzis. This, combined with the British ship's faster rate of fire, made them a particularly deadly opponent.

An AP shell fired from an Italian 15.2cm/53 gun had a broadly similar performance, particularly after muzzle velocity was reduced to 850mps during 1940–41 in an attempt to improve accuracy. Armour penetration was estimated at 8.6cm at 14,000m, with a similar longer range plunging fire performance, penetrating 4.5cm of deck armour at 18,000m. This meant that while the thickest box protection of most British cruisers might not be penetrated, the rest of the ship and the deck armour remained vulnerable. So, the similar gunnery capabilities of the light cruisers in both fleets made them equally effective – and susceptible. This meant that victory in any naval engagement would rely more on the tactical situation, the professionalism of the officers and men and the calibre of naval commanders than on the technical nuances of gunnery, ballistics and armour.

THE COMBATANTS

BRITISH AND COMMONWEALTH CRUISER CREWS

Before the war, the Royal Navy's ships were manned by highly trained regular seamen, many of whom had many years of experience. Following the outbreak of war, these regulars were joined by naval reservists, who often had years of training under their belts. Those who lacked this depth of knowledge made up for it with enthusiasm and a willingness to learn. During the war, they were joined by Hostilities Only ratings, called up for the duration of the conflict. These were quickly assimilated and taught their new profession. Fortunately, they had expert instructors in their officers, non-commissioned officers and regular shipmates. The result was that by 1940, for the most part, the crews of British or Commonwealth warships deployed in the Mediterranean could be relied upon to deal with whatever challenges they faced.

Part of this reliability stemmed from their leaders. The commissioned and non-commissioned officers of the pre-war navy were invariably thorough-going professionals and often experts in their field, whether it be gunnery, seamanship, engineering or aviation. Before the war, the Mediterranean Fleet was known for its high professional standards, created through a combination of frequent exercises and fleet manoeuvres. The same was true during the war, as the theatre was considered a particularly challenging one, and required high standards of training. So, while Admiral Cunningham continued to carry out fleet training and exercises in the Eastern

The Engine Room of a British cruiser. During deployments in the Mediterranean the stokers would often have to work in these uncomfortably hot, cramped spaces, and in action there was the ever-present risk of being trapped there if the ship was hit.

In December 1940 the light cruiser *Manchester* took part in the Battle of Spartivento, but afterwards she returned Britain for a refit. She was back in the Mediterranean the following June, and on 23 July she was badly damaged by an aerial torpedo, while operating in support of a Malta convoy. This shows her damage repair teams on her quarterdeck, recovering between spells below decks, trying to save their ship. In the end, *Manchester* made it back to Gibraltar.

Mediterranean, where possible, ships deployed there also underwent short, intensive training programmes beforehand. That way their ships' companies were at the peak of efficiency.

During this period the fleet was stretched thinly, with demands on it coming from the Home Fleet, and from commitments ranging from the protection of Atlantic and Arctic convoys to the defence of British and Commonwealth interests in the Far East. So, cruisers could be sent to the theatre when newly commissioned, after completing repairs in either British or American shipyards, or when redeployed from other fleets or theatres such as the Home Fleet or the Eastern Fleet. In theory, these warships had a home port – Portsmouth, Devonport (Plymouth) or Chatham for British ships, and Sydney for Australian ones. This is where manpower and welfare requirements were managed, spare parts were stored and where many of the crews' families lived. However, a deployment to the Mediterranean involved a lengthy separation from families and from the logistical support offered by a home port.

British and Commonwealth cruisers often remained in commission for lengthy periods, and some of them spent years in the Mediterranean theatre. Before the summer of 1940, the Mediterranean Fleet had primarily been based in Malta, a base with the repair facilities, stores and support facilities needed to keep the fleet in operation. The coming of war with Italy meant the fleet was

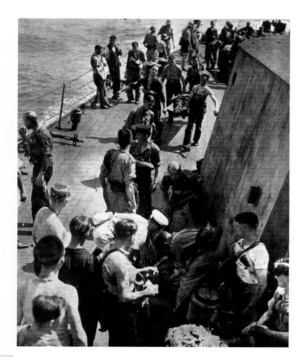

ADMIRAL ANDREW BROWNE CUNNINGHAM (1883–1963)

Cunningham, known widely in the Service as 'ABC' after his initials, took command of the Mediterranean Fleet in June 1939, after a spell at the Admiralty. He joined the navy at 15, and first saw action ashore during the Boer War. During World War I, he commanded a destroyer in the Mediterranean, saw action again off the Dardanelles and ended the war as a decorated commander. He commanded a destroyer during the Baltic Campaign of 1918–19, and on his return home he was promoted and given command of a destroyer flotilla. He went on to command a cruiser and a battleship, and reached flag rank in 1932. Subsequent commands included command of the Mediterranean Fleet's destroyers and then second in command of the fleet. This meant he was a highly experienced Mediterranean hand.

When war came, Cunningham used his charm and diplomatic skill to convince Vice Admiral Godfroy to agree to the peaceful internment of his French squadron. His greatest challenge though, lay in establishing control of the Mediterranean. As a fleet commander he showed innovation in initiating the air attack on Taranto, aggression in his pursuit of the Italian battle fleet at Calabria and Spartivento and cunning in formulating the trap he laid at Matapan. He also showed determination to the point of recklessness during the naval battles around Crete. Above all, though, Cunningham was able to delegate, and so he gave subordinates considerable leeway, leaving him free to coordinate the often large-scale operations that wore down the combat resolve of the Regia Marina. Promoted to admiral of the fleet in 1943, he went on to oversee the Allied landings in Sicily and Italy and the surrender of the Italian battle fleet. He subsequently served as First Sea Lord until he returned from the service in 1946.

Admiral Cunningham was a hugely gifted commander, who successfully thwarted Axis attempts to deny his fleet control of the Mediterranean Sea. (Imperial War Museums via Getty Images)

relocated to Alexandria in Egypt, a port that initially lacked many of these facilities and provided fewer recreational facilities for the crew. For many ships, the only respite came when the cruiser was sent home for a refit or to be repaired. Then the crew would be temporarily decommissioned, and sent on leave. In many cases, recommissioning involved a largely fresh crew, who needed to learn the ways of their new ship before she could be restored to peak efficiency.

Above all, for the sailors who crewed these cruisers, deployment in the Mediterranean was often a dangerous one, particularly if the ship was involved in the hard-fought naval battles around Crete or in the waters around Malta, or in the bitterly contested Malta convoys. In the Mediterranean, the almost constant risk of attack by land-based aircraft or enemy submarines meant that the pressure was rarely off, and relief only came when the ship safely returned to Gibraltar or Alexandria. These challenges were usually met with the professionalism, cheerful resilience, sense of humour and can-do attitude which came to epitomize the wartime British or Commonwealth sailor. Without men of this calibre at his disposal, Admiral Cunningham might have had a very different fight on his hands.

ITALIAN CRUISER CREWS

The Italian dictator Benito Mussolini, inspecting the crew of the battleship *Littorio* as it lay in Taranto during the summer of 1942. Unlike Hitler, he understood the rudiments of seapower, and so concentrated his fleet's limited resources in an effort to protect Italy's vital convoy routes to Greece and Libya.

During the 1930s the manpower of the Regia Marina expanded steadily, so that by June 1940 it numbered over 168,000 officers and men. This was twice its September 1939 strength and three times its level in June 1935. This increase was achieved through a mixture of conscription and voluntary enlistment. Volunteers were attracted by steady pay and the teaching of useful skills during their four-year enlistment. By mid-1940, these volunteers made up approximately half of the navy's manpower, with the rest of the force divided fairly equally between old regular sailors and conscripts.

At the time, Italy did not have universal education, and lacked a large, skilled industrial workforce. So, compared to their Royal Naval counterparts these new sailors were, for the most part, less literate, less technically adept and less able to absorb the detailed intricacies of modern warships.

This in turn placed a greater emphasis on the abilities of the Regia Marina's commissioned and non-commissioned officers. The Regia Marina boasted a well-trained officer corps, many of whom were trained in the more technical aspects of their profession. These officers tended to be well motivated and professional, but as a body they tended towards conservative values. So, for the most part they remained loyal to their king rather than to the Italian Fascist government. This, though, also

AMMIRAGLIO DI SQUADRA ANGELO IACHINO (1889–1976)

When World War II began, Ammiraglio di Squadra (Vice Admiral) Angelo Iachino was a member of the naval staff, having been promoted the previous September, and commander of the naval academy in Livorno. However, in July he was given command of the Regia Marina's Seconda Squadra (2nd Squadron), based in Taranto – a mixed force of cruisers and destroyers. Before the end of the year, he was given command of the entire battle fleet. The son of a schoolteacher, Iachino joined the navy at 15, and first went to sea on board the battleship *Regina Margherita*. For much of World War I he served on the dreadnought *Giulio Cesare*, but in 1918 he was given command of a torpedo boat, and saw action during an attack on the Austro-Hungarian naval base at Pola. After the war he went on to command a gunboat in the Far East, and other commands followed, including the Cadorna-class light cruiser *Armando Diaz*. In 1936 he was promoted to flag rank, and was promoted again three years later. His ultimate test, though, was as the commander of the Squadra Navale.

He had already commanded the Seconda Squadra at Spartivento, but following his elevation to Commander-in-Chief of the Italian Battle Fleet on 9 December 1940, Iachino found himself commanding both squadrons, combined into a single entity. It was a post Iachino would hold until April 1943. The following April, despite his misgivings, Iachino led his fleet into action in the operation that ended in disaster off Matapan. He was eventually given a little more operational latitude, and possibly as a result of this, his fleet performed more successfully at the two battles of Sirte in December 1941 and March 1942. It was Iachino who organized the protection of the Libyan convoys in the face of attacks by Force K, and who, in June 1942, forced the withdrawal of a British convoy to Malta. Throughout his period in command Iachino showed his willingness to use aggressive tactics, and this, combined with his clear grasp of often complex naval operations, made him a formidable opponent. The following April he was promoted, and handed over his command to Ammiraglio di Squadra Carlo Bergamini. However, it was Iachino, more than any other Italian commander, who would bring out the best in the ships and men under his command.

Iachino (upper left) was one of the more gifted senior officers in the Regia Marina. While he oversaw the debacle at Matapan in 1941, he went on to show greater skill at the battles of Sirte and operations against westbound Malta convoys.

The Zara-class heavy cruiser *Gorizia*, pictured in her base port of Taranto, while some of her crew enjoy an al fresco communal shower on the quayside. During late 1941, the cruiser served as part of the escort for the Libyan convoys, which were preyed upon by Malta's Force K.

encouraged them to maintain a distinct social separation from their men, which over time proved detrimental to morale. Non-commissioned officers were drawn from the ranks of the old regular navy or else recruited from among the volunteers, who were then trained as artificers and technical specialists. The same lack of technical expertise among these men meant that it took time to train them to the level the navy required. In the interim, any shortfall in expertise had to be made up by the ship's officers.

As the war continued, it became apparent that morale in the fleet was high, despite a number of setbacks, but the fleet's senior officers often lacked the initiative needed to take full advantage of a tactical situation, as they felt constrained by a combination of doctrine, bureaucracy and cautious, restrictive orders. For the same reason they often lacked the aggression found in British cruiser commanders such as Pridham-Wippell, Tovey or Vian. So, opportunities were wasted or lost and the Regia Marina's critics were able to describe the Italians as 'battle-shy'. This was certainly not the case – less senior officers often displayed commendable skill and aggression in action. The same was true on individual ships – on the whole, Italian cruisers were fortunate in their officers, who shouldered much of the burden for maintaining the operational efficiency of their ships.

One problem faced by the Regia Marina was a by-product of geography. The fleet tended to spend less time at sea than its British and Commonwealth counterparts, as for the most part Italy's cruisers were used to accompany the battle fleet or to support convoy operations between Italy and Libya. Increasingly, the battleships stayed in port, and it was left to the cruisers to provide heavy cover for these convoys. In all, between the outbreak of war and the armistice of September 1943, the fleet's cruisers spent 669 days at sea, steaming 383,814 nautical miles in the process. This was four times the total of the fleet's battleships, but with operations lasting less than a week at a time, sea time was limited. Instead, cruisers spent long periods in port. This made it harder to hone the ship's company into an efficient fighting unit, and for the men to gain practical seagoing experience. For everyone from the captain to the lookouts, this made it harder to gain the skills needed to make their ship as efficient and combat-ready as those of their veteran adversaries.

THE FLEETS

In June 1940 the Royal Navy's strength in the Mediterranean was concentrated at Alexandria, the home base of Admiral Cunningham's Mediterranean Fleet. Smaller naval forces were deployed at Gibraltar and Malta. At the time, the Mediterranean Fleet consisted of four battleships, an aircraft carrier, eight light cruisers, 22 destroyers and six submarines. Force H, based in Gibraltar, was made up of a battlecruiser, an aircraft carrier and a light cruiser, supported by nine destroyers. A second flotilla of six submarines was based in Malta, while a force of four light cruisers and four destroyers was on patrol in the Red Sea.

At the time, Admiral Campione's battle fleet based at Taranto was made up of two battleships, seven heavy cruisers, 12 light cruisers and 40 destroyers. Another two older light cruisers (*Bari* and *Taranto*) and six destroyers were on patrol in the Adriatic, and four more destroyers were based at Benghazi, together with the old armoured cruiser *San Giorgio*, while two more destroyers were in the Aegean, and seven in the Red Sea. The bulk of Italy's 113-strong submarine fleet was concentrated in the Western Mediterranean, but smaller flotillas operated in the Aegean, the Red Sea and in Libya.

As the war progressed, cruiser numbers fluctuated continually, as more British warships were deployed to the Mediterranean, or were damaged, sunk or sent elsewhere. The Italians, of course, were permanently stationed in the Central Mediterranean, and their ships were also damaged and withdrawn from service to be repaired, or were sunk. The following table traces this varied British deployment. A number of British or Commonwealth cruisers are not listed below as they never participated in the war in the Mediterranean.

In 1940–41 the Leander-class light cruiser *Orion* served as the flagship of Rear Admiral Tovey's 7th Cruiser Squadron and then Vice Admiral Pridham-Wippell's Force X. She saw extensive action, fighting at Calabria, Otranto and Matapan. However, on 29 May 1941 she was badly damaged during an air attack off Crete, which put her out of action until early 1943.

British heavy cruisers		
Ship	Class	
Berwick	Kent	Early November to late November 1940
Kent		Mid-June to mid-September 1940, when damaged
York	York	Mid-July 1940 until her wrecking on 26 March 1941

British light cruisers		
Ship	Class	
Caledon	Caledon	June 1940 to July 1941, August 1944 to March 1945
Coventry	Ceres	August to December 1940, March 1941 until her loss on 14 September 1942
Capetown	Carlisle	June 1940 to March 1941
Delhi	D class	June to September 1940, November 1942, July 1943 to February 1944
Despatch		November 1940
Dragon		March to May 1940
Emerald	E class	June 1940

Ship	Class	Service Period
Leander	Leander	Early June to late October 1941
Orion		Mid-March 1940 to late May 1941, then January 1943 to May 1944, and August 1944 until end of war
Neptune		May to November 1940, then October 1941 until her loss on 19 December 1941
Ajax		Mid-July 1940 to mid-February 1942
Arethusa	Arethusa	June 1940 to April 1941, July to November 1941, April to November 1942, then January 1945 until end of war
Aurora		September 1941 to March 1942, July 1942 to October 1943, April 1944 to end of war
Galatea		July 1941 until her loss on 14 December 1941
Penelope		October to December 1941, February 1943 until her loss on 18 February 1944
Hobart	Perth	August to December 1941
Perth		December 1940 to May 1941, June to July 1941
Sydney		June 1940 to January 1941
Birmingham	Southampton	June 1942, November 1943
Glasgow		November to December 1940
Gloucester		June 1940 until her loss on 22 May 1941
Liverpool		June to October 1940, June 1942
Manchester		Mid-September to December 1940, July 1941, August 1943 until her loss on 13 August 1943
Newcastle		Early November to December 1940, June 1941
Sheffield		August to October 1940, January to October 1941, November 1942, September 1943
Southampton		November 1940, January 1941 until her loss on 11 January 1941
Edinburgh	Edinburgh	July to September 1941
Fiji	Fiji	April 1941 until her loss on 22 May 1941
Kenya		September to October 1941, June to August 1942
Mauritius		April to September 1943, October 1943 to February 1944
Newfoundland		May to July 1943
Nigeria		August 1942
Jamaica		November 1942
Uganda		July to September 1943

British AA cruisers		
Ship	Class	
Cairo	Carlisle	Early May 1942 until her loss on 12 August 1942
Calcutta		Mid-August 1940 until her loss on 1 June 1941
Carlisle		September 1940 to October 1943
Colombo		Mid-March 1943 until early November 1944
Argonaut	Dido	Late November to December 1942, then August 1944 until end of war
Bonaventure		Mid-January 1941 until her loss on 31 March 1941
Charybdis		April 1942 until mid-October 1943
Cleopatra		Early January 1942 until mid-July 1943
Dido		April 1941, then December 1941 to April 1943, and June 1943 to July 1944
Euryalus		Mid-September 1941 to early October 1943
Hermione		Lost in June 1942
Naiad		May 1941 until her loss on 11 March 1942
Phoebe		April to late August 1941, then May to September 1942, and July 1943 to June 1944
Scylla		October to December 1942, then September to October 1943
Sirius		August 1942 to October 1943, then August 1944 until end of war
Black Prince	Mod Dido	August to October 1944
Royalist		August to November 1944
Spartan		December 1943 until her loss on 29 January 1944

A rare photograph of Vice Admiral Cattaneo's 1st Division at sea, on the eve of the Battle of Matapan. His flagship Zara is followed in line astern by Pola and Fiume, with Abruzzi in the foreground. The picture was taken from Garibaldi. All three of the heavy cruisers would be sunk during the battle.

As all of these Italian cruisers were deployed permanently in the theatre, so the following list reflects periods when these ships were *not* in operational service.

Italian heavy cruisers		
Ship	Class	
Trento	Trento	Served until loss on 15 June 1942
Trieste		Under repair late November 1941 to early June 1942, lost on 11 April 1943
Zara	Zara	Under repair late October to early December 1940, lost on 29 March 1941
Pola		Under repair mid-December 1940 to late February 1941, lost on 29 March 1941
Fiume		Served until loss on 29 March 1941
Gorizia		Under repair late November 1941, early June 1942, and from mid-April 1943 until armistice
Bolzano	Bolzano	Under repair late June to early July 1940, late August 1941 to early July 1942, and from mid-August 1942 until armistice

Italian light cruisers		
Ship	Class	
Bande Nere	da Giussano	Served until loss on 1 April 1942
da Barbiano		Refit early September 1940 to early March 1941, then training duties until early December. Lost on 13 December 1941
Colleoni		Served until loss on 19 July 1940
da Giussano		Served until loss on 13 December 1941
Cadorna	Cadorna	In reserve from mid-February to late June 1941, and from January 1942 to May 1943, then refit until mid-June.
Diaz		Served until loss on 25 February 1941
Attendolo	Montecuccoli	Under repair late August 1942 until loss on 4 December
Montecuccoli		Served until armistice
Duca d'Aosta	Duca d'Aosta	Served until armistice
Eugenio di Savoia		Under repair late December 1942 to July 1943, then served until armistice
Duca degli Abruzzi	Abruzzi	Under repair late November 1941 to June 1942, then served until armistice
Garibaldi		Under repair late April to early November 1941

COMBAT

During the long, hard-fought naval campaign in the Mediterranean, battleships or aircraft carriers weren't the arbiters of victory. They certainly had their uses – the air strike on Taranto in November 1940 and the nocturnal naval clash off Cape Matapan in March 1941 demonstrated that. These actions, though, were rarities. Instead, the bulk of the fighting was left to cruisers and destroyers, producing a string of clashes which illustrate the effectiveness of these warships in action. Setting purely destroyer actions aside, the majority of these clashes weren't even between rival cruiser forces, although they did happen. Instead, most were between cruisers and destroyers, or against well-protected convoys. The cruisers of both sides fell prey to enemy submarines, or to mines. Then, particularly for the cruisers of the Royal Navy, the greatest threat came from the air. During the Crete campaign, or the Malta convoys, these cruisers faced air attacks of unprecedented ferocity, and several of the warships succumbed to German or Italian bombs and torpedoes.

The aim of this chapter is not to examine all of these clashes, but to offer a glimpse into the range of combat situations in which these cruisers were placed. That way we

In October 1941 the Arethusa-class light cruiser *Aurora*, commanded by Captain 'Bill' Agnew arrived in Malta, where she became the flagship of Agnew's Force K. This Malta Striking Force enjoyed considerable success, but after hitting a mine in December, *Aurora* was sent home for repairs.

can better evaluate how the ships and their crews measured up to the challenge. In the process we can gain a better understanding of just how versatile cruisers were – especially light ones – and how they were employed in a surprisingly wide range of missions during the campaign. It is also worth pointing out that in June 1940, at the start of the battle for the Mediterranean, both the Royal Navy and the Regia Marina fully expected to face a large-scale sea battle, the outcome of which would decide the mastery of the Mediterranean. When this failed to materialize, cruisers were increasingly detached from the rival battle fleets and formed into semi-independent commands. These were better suited to the kind of war that developed in the theatre, and made the most of the fighting potential of these powerful warships.

SWEEPS AND CONVOY ATTACKS

One of the first encounters was on 28 June, barely two weeks after the conflict began. That evening, the five ships of Vice Admiral Tovey's 7th Cruiser Squadron were at sea to the west of Crete when they encountered Captain Baroni's 2nd Destroyer Squadron. Baroni's own destroyer *Espero* was slower than her two escorts, so he ordered them to escape while he covered them with smoke, then he turned to engage the British. *Orion* managed to 'comb' her torpedoes, but *Espero* scored a hit, damaging *Liverpool* above the waterline. *Neptune* and Tovey's flagship *Orion* pounded the Italian destroyer, then left the Australian *Sydney* to finish her off. Tovey's squadron wasted precious ammunition sinking a solitary destroyer, at a time when the fleet's pre-war shell stocks were dangerously low.

By contrast *Ajax* distinguished herself off Cape Passero early on 12 October when she encountered a force of Italian destroyers and torpedo boats to the east of Malta. Captain McCarthy's cruiser dodged a torpedo salvo to sink one torpedo boat and cripple another, which later that morning was finished off by *York*. The rest of the Italian force broke contact. This small action demonstrated that the Royal Navy had the edge in night-fighting – something the Italians had rarely practised before the war. A string of similar actions would follow over the coming months, such as clashes in the Sicilian Narrows (November 1940), off Pantelleria (January 1941), and the *Lupo* and *Sagittario* convoy actions (both May 1941). In each case, a force of British light cruisers, sometimes supported by destroyers, successfully engaged lighter convoy escorts, or drove off attacks on British convoys. Incidentally, during the *Lupo* convoy attack off north-west Crete, *Orion* also narrowly missed being torpedoed. *Orion*, *Ajax* and *Dido* also went on to sink over half the convoy of small caïques, filled with crack German mountain troops.

The use of a mixed force of light cruisers and destroyers also proved effective elsewhere. Early on 12 November 1940, Vice Admiral Pridham-Wippell's Force X, made up of three light cruisers (*Orion*, *Sydney* and *Ajax*) and two destroyers encountered an Italian convoy while sweeping the Strait of Otranto. One escorting armed merchant cruiser was damaged and another driven off. Force X then fell upon the convoy, sinking all four of its ships. It marked the first night-attack on an Italian convoy, and showed just how deadly these could be. In late 1941, Captain Agnew,

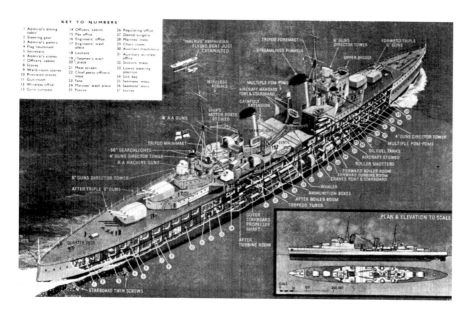

KEY TO NUMBERS

1 Admiral's dining cabin
2 Steering gear
3 Admiral's pantry
4 Flag lieutenant
5 Secretary
6 Admiral's stores
7 Officers' cabins
8 Stores
9 Ward-room stores
10 Provision stores
11 Gun-room
12 Wireless office
13 Gyro compass
14 Officers' cabins
15 Pay office
16 Engineers' office
17 Engineers' wash place
18 Lockers
19 Seamen's wash place
20 Lockers
21 Mess screen
22 Chief petty officers' mess
23 Fans
24 Marines' wash place
25 Pantry
26 Regulating office
27 Dental surgery
28 Marines' mess
29 Chart room
30 Auxiliary machinery
31 Auxiliary wireless office
32 Stokers' mess
33 Lower steering position
34 Sick bay
35 Seamens' mess
36 Seamens' mess
37 Stores

This diagram of a Southampton-class light cruiser was produced by the Admiralty during the war as a part of a publicity exercise. It highlights just how much of the hull space was taken up by the ship's propulsion systems.

commanding Force K – a small mixed force of cruisers and destroyers based in Malta – would achieve further successes against small Libyan convoys, driving off weaker escorts to sink the convoy's merchantmen. On 9 November, Agnew even risked an attack on a convoy escorted by a much larger escort, including two heavy cruisers.

In early November, the Beta Convoy of seven ships left Naples, bound for Tripoli. An unusually powerful escort was provided for it, which included Rear Admiral Brivonesi's 3rd Cruiser Division, *Trieste* and *Trento*, as well as nine destroyers. A little after midnight on 9 November 1941, after detecting the enemy on radar, Force K attacked it from the west. Agnew's flagship *Aurora* led the attack, followed in line by a destroyer, then *Penelope* and a second destroyer. The British relied on surprise to win the fight, and radar. Two Italian destroyers were hit, forcing the convoy to turn away. The Italian covering force, some miles astern, wasn't informed, and so the two heavy cruisers and three destroyers remained oblivious to them. This allowed Agnew to concentrate his fire on the convoy.

It took less than 90 minutes to drive off the destroyer close escort and then sink the entire convoy. Brivonesi's cruisers could have saved the merchantmen, but instead they continued on to the south, and so Agnew sped off northwards, leaving the blazing wreckage of the convoy behind him. It was a brilliantly executed attack, and showed what determination, surprise and good leadership could achieve, especially if the attackers had the advantage of radar. Afterwards, Brivonesi was relieved of his command and set ashore to command a backwater naval base. The escort commander, Captain Bisciani, was also censured. Italy's woes continued when, on 13 December, the light cruisers *da Barbiano* and *da Giussano* were sunk off Cape Bon in Tunisia in a night clash with four of Force K's destroyers. The following summer, the Italians would show that they too could carry out an audacious surprise attack on a well-defended convoy.

During Operation *Harpoon*, the fighting through of a well-protected convoy to Malta, the Regia Marina tried to repeat Force K's success. First, the convoy was

The reason the Axis convoys to North Africa were so important was that they were the only means of supplying or reinforcing the German and Italian troops there that formed part of Rommel's forces. Here a Pz. II tank, earmarked for the Afrika Corps, is unloaded onto the quayside in Tripoli.

subjected to a succession of heavy air attacks. Once the convoy reached the Sicilian Narrows, the heavier escorts returned to Gibraltar, leaving a reduced escort to accompany the convoy on to Malta. Late on 13 June Rear Admiral Da Zara's flagship *Eugenio di Savoia* left Cagliari, accompanied by the *Montecuccoli* and five destroyers. Early the following morning Da Zara began his attack, opening fire at a range of 7½ miles. The escorts, the old anti-aircraft cruiser *Cairo* and two destroyers were damaged, as was an Italian destroyer. A running fight developed, and *Cairo* was hit again. The cruisers' attack also contributed to the loss of the destroyer *Bedouin*, their fire distracting her crew while she was being attacked by torpedo bombers. The action continued until mid-afternoon when, with his cruisers running low on ammunition, Da Zara broke off the attack. The operation, arguably the most spirited Italian cruiser action of the war, was deemed a moderate success, and it could have been much more so if the Italian Air Force had been willing to liaise with the Navy, so air and surface attacks could be coordinated. This lack of air force cooperation was a problem that would plague the Regia Marina throughout the war.

INITIAL CLASHES

Strangely, there were relatively few instances of cruisers meeting and fighting their enemy counterparts. Probably the most dramatic of these took place off Cape Spada in Crete on 19 July 1940. In mid-July, Rear Admiral Casardi was sent from Tripoli to the Aegean to intercept two British tankers. His flagship *Giovanni delle Bande Nere* was accompanied by *Bartolomeo Colleoni*. That morning, as he entered the Antikithera Strait, he encountered a patrolling flotilla of British destroyers. He gave chase, and the two sides exchanged long-range fire. Suddenly, at 0730hrs gun flashes were spotted to the north. It was *Sydney*. Casardi turned away and made smoke, and *Sydney* and the

A reproduction of a painting by Lieutenant-Commander Rowland Langmaid, a member of Cunningham's staff, showing Admiral Pridham-Wippell's 15th Cruiser Squadron in action off Gavdos before Matapan, on the morning of 28 March 1941. From left to right it shows *Orion*, *Ajax*, *Perth* and *Gloucester*.

British destroyers duly gave chase. Casardi hoped to use his ship's superior speed to pull away, but first he had to clear Cape Spada, to enter the Cretan Sea.

The three cruisers exchanged fire, and both *Sydney* and *Bande Nere* suffered minor hits. Then, at 0825hrs, *Bartolomeo Colleoni* received rudder and boiler hits, which effectively left her dead in the water. She was finished off by a torpedo fired from the British destroyer *Ilex*. Casardi realized he could do nothing to help, and so gave the order to break off the action. With the sinking of *Bartolomeo Colleoni*, the Regia Marina had lost the first of its modern cruisers. In the enquiry that followed, the Supermarina concluded that the exceptionally light armour of the da Giussano class had made her especially vulnerable, particularly when deployed in waters dominated by the enemy. However, the real lesson was that adequate air reconnaissance may have prevented Casardi from stumbling into the *Sydney*.

Ten days before this, the British and Italian battle fleets had clashed for the first time, 50 nautical miles off the Punta Stilo, in Calabria. This meeting in the Ionian Sea was largely a chance affair, as both battle fleets had been covering convoys. The battle began on 8 July, when a series of mass air attacks were thrown against the British fleet. The only serious damage, though, was to the light cruiser *Gloucester*, when a bomb struck her bridge. Admiral Campioni turned north to engage Cunningham's fleet, and just after 1500hrs the following afternoon, lookouts on *Neptune* spotted the approaching enemy fleet. Shortly afterwards, the Italians

British cruisers in action at the Battle of Spartivento, 27 November 1940. Two Southampton-class light cruisers can be seen in the foreground, with the heavy cruiser *Berwick*, Vice Admiral Holland's flagship, in the distance.

opened fire on the nearest British ships – Tovey's 7th Cruiser Squadron. This opening long-range skirmish saw *Neptune* hit by shells from *Garibaldi*, fired at a range of ten miles.

Soon, though, the rival battleships had come within range. At around 1600hrs, the Italian flagship *Giulio Cesare* was hit by a 15in. shell from *Warspite*. This encouraged Campioni to break off the action, using his heavy cruisers to cover the disengagement, and to send in a destroyer attack to prevent the British from giving chase. The Battle of Calabria (or Punta Stilo) was more of a short skirmish than a real fleet action, but at least Tovey's 7th Cruiser Squadron, comprising *Orion* (flag), *Neptune*, *Sydney* and *Liverpool*, managed to trade shots with the Italian 4th and 8th Divisions' *da Barbiano*, *da Giussano*, *Abruzzi* and *Garibaldi*. The battle began to wind down after Campioni's battleships broke contact, but by 1400hrs a running fight had developed as the rest of the fleets continued northwards on near parallel courses. During this second skirmish, *Trento* engaged *Warspite*, and straddled her at the extreme range of 14 miles. It was impressive shooting. At 1605hrs, a 6in. shell from *Neptune* struck *Bolzano*, jamming her rudder and detonating several torpedoes.

Minutes later, six Swordfish biplanes from *Eagle* tried unsuccessfully to torpedo *Bolzano* and *Trento*. With that the Italians broke off under cover of an equally unproductive torpedo attack by the Italian destroyers. While the Battle of Calabria was inconclusive, it gave both sides the opportunity to test the accuracy of their gunnery. The British observed that Italian cruiser fire was accurate in terms of range, but less so in precision. This problem would continue for much of the war. The next fleet clash at the Battle of Cape Spartivento (or Capo Teulada) allowed the rival cruisers to test their mettle even more. That November, the Italian battle fleet sortied to prevent a small but vital British eastbound convoy from reaching Malta. The convoy was covered by Somerville's Force H. In the early afternoon of 27 November, the two fleets clashed some 40 miles south of Sardinia.

This time, Campioni's fleet comprised two battleships, six heavy cruisers and 14 destroyers, while Somerville commanded a battleship, a battlecruiser, a heavy cruiser, four light cruisers and ten destroyers. The clash began at 1230hrs when the rival cruisers engaged each other at a range of 12 miles. *Berwick* was hit twice by *Pola*, knocking out the Y turret, so she pulled out of the British line. The British light cruisers kept closing the range, though, with *Manchester*, *Sheffield* and *Newcastle* engaging *Trieste* with their forward turrets, while *Southampton* targeted *Fiume*. Vice Admiral Holland's cruisers kept getting closer, forcing Campioni to order his own cruisers to turn away. The two groups of cruisers now ran towards the north-east, exchanging fire as they went. *Trieste*, *Trento* and *Bolzano* were 12 miles from the British cruisers, while *Pola*, *Fiume* and *Gorizia* were four miles closer. A Swordfish attack on Campioni's flagship *Vittorio Veneto* encouraged the Italian commander to break contact, and shortly after 1300hrs both sides had ceased fire. However, this second inconclusive battle could have ended differently if Campioni had held his nerve. The following month he was moved to the Supermarina, and Vice Admiral Iachino took over command of his fleet.

In February 1942 the brand-new Dido-class cruiser Cleopatra was damaged by a bomb on her first mission – the protection of a Malta convoy. After being repaired in Gibraltar she was sent to Alexandria, becoming the flagship of Rear Admiral Vian's 15th Cruiser Squadron. She saw action at the Second Battle of Sirte, before taking part in the *Pedestal* convoy operation, before leading Force K in attacks on Axis convoys bound for Tunisia.

LATER ACTIONS

The next time the two cruiser forces clashed was on 28 March 1941. The previous winter the Italians had attacked Greece, and when the campaign stalled, Germany had to send a sizeable number of troops southwards into the Balkans. Britain stood by Greece, and so troops were shipped there from North Africa. In late March, the Italian battle fleet put to sea, to sweep the area west of Crete for these convoys. Instead, they ran into Cunningham's Mediterranean Fleet. At 0720hrs that morning, a reconnaissance aircraft from *Formidable* sighted three Italian cruisers to the south of Cape Matapan, but missed the rest of the battle fleet. Pridham-Wippell's 15th Cruiser Division (*Orion*, *Ajax*, *Perth* and *Gloucester*) was sent to intercept them, and 40 minutes later the two sides made contact. Vice Admiral Sansonetti's 3rd Division (*Trieste*, *Trento* and *Bolzano*) opened at a range of 13½ miles, and Pridham-Wippell turned and ran south, towards Cunningham. Sansonetti gave chase, but broke it off at 0830hrs. The British later described the Italian fire as accurate but slow, and becoming more ineffective as time wore on.

Admiral Iachino, commanding the Italian battle fleet, decided to return to port, but throughout the afternoon his ships were harassed by British carrier strikes. Just before dark, *Pola* was hit and she lost power. Iachino's flagship, *Vittorio Veneto*, was also damaged. Iachino detached the rest of Vice Admiral Cattaneo's 1st Cruiser Division (*Zara* and *Fiume*) along with four destroyers to assist *Pola*, and bring her safely into port. He then continued to steam away to the west. Later that evening, Cunningham's

Vice Admiral James Somerville (1882–1949) commanded Force H from the summer of 1940 until the spring of 1942, when he was promoted and given command of the Eastern Fleet. So, it was Somerville's responsibility to push through and protect the eastbound Malta convoys in the face of heavy attacks from both sea and air.

PREVIOUS PAGES
**The Battle of Pantelleria,
15 June 1942.**
By the summer of 1942, the
Central Mediterranean was firmly
controlled by the Axis. However,
as the beleaguered island
fortress of Malta was desperately
short of supplies, the Admiralty
agreed to send two small but
well-protected convoys to Malta,
one from Alexandria and the other
from Gibraltar. The eastbound
convoy, MW-4, sailed on 12 June.
Two days later it was subjected to
heavy air attacks as it entered
the narrow strait between Sicily
and the coast of Tunisia. These
attacks continued the following
day, 15 June, but this time these
coincided with a surface attack
spearheaded by Rear Admiral Da
Zara's 7th Cruiser Division. His
force consisted of the light
cruisers *Eugenio di Savoia* and
Raimondo Montecuccoli and six
destroyers. The convoy's close
escort of one old AA cruiser, five
destroyers and four destroyer
escorts was outnumbered and
outgunned. Still, it laid smoke to
cover the merchantmen, and
fought back. In the running battle
that followed, the destroyer
Bedouin was sunk, *Cairo* and the
destroyer *Partridge* damaged,
and two merchant ships sunk,
including a precious tanker.
This shows the action soon after
dawn at 0540hrs, when the
Italian flagship *Eugenio di Savoia*
and the *Raimondo Montecuccoli*
(pictured here) first engaged
Cairo, nine miles away to the
west, on a parallel southerly
course.

battleships detected the Italian cruisers on radar and closed in for the kill. Three British battleships positioned themselves to within point-blank range, and shortly after 2230hrs they opened fire. The Italians were taken completely by surprise, and their cruisers were torn apart, together with two escorting destroyers. British observers noted that the enemy's guns were still trained fore and aft. For the Regia Marina, the Battle of Matapan was an unmitigated disaster.

In late 1941, the increased pace of the conflict in North Africa meant a greater role for Axis convoys. So, in mid-December the four-ship Convoy M42 sailed from Taranto, bound for Tripoli. Its covering force included two battleships and the cruisers *Gorizia* and *Trento*. The British were also at sea, escorting the merchantman *Breconshire* to Malta. When Cunningham learned of the Italian convoy, he ordered his escort commander, Rear Admiral Vian, to attack it. Vian's force was made up of *Naiad* and *Euryalus* from his own squadron, Force K's *Aurora* and *Penelope* and 12 destroyers. In the clash on 17 December, known as the First Battle of Sirte, the two cruiser forces encountered each other some 200 nautical miles north-west of Benghazi. Rear Admiral Parona's two cruisers were well ahead of the convoy and the battleships. Spotting them, Vian ordered Force K to protect *Breconshire*, and closed with the enemy. Parona's cruisers opened fire at 16 miles, but no hits were scored before Vian broke off under cover of a smoke screen. As they withdrew, one British destroyer was slightly damaged. Both the *Breconshire* and Convoy M42 made it safely into port.

Three months later on 22 March the Second Battle of Sirte was fought in roughly the same area. It involved a determined Italian attack on a four-ship convoy bound from Alexandria to Malta. After it was spotted, Iachino put to sea in his flagship *Littorio*, accompanied by Parona's three cruisers (*Gorizia*, *Trento* and *Bande Nere*) and seven destroyers. That afternoon, in gale-force conditions, Parona's cruisers were sighted by *Euryalus*, part of Vian's 15th Cruiser Squadron, which also included *Cleopatra* and *Dido*. Parona opened fire at 11½ miles – the limit of visibility. The British convoy turned away, screened by Vian and his accompanying destroyers. A running battle followed, with no hits being scored on either side until 1643hrs, when a shell from *Bande Nere* struck the bridge of Vian's flagship *Cleopatra*.

Minutes later, when *Littorio* came into action, and the convoy came under air attack, Vian sent in a destroyer flotilla to force the Italian battleship to turn away. No torpedo hits were scored, but Iachino turned away, and the, by then, battered destroyers broke contact. Vian's convoy made it safely into Malta the following day – where the ships were duly sunk by Axis bombers. Both sides had shown spirit during the action, but again neither side managed to land a decisive blow.

The Second Battle of Sirte proved to be the last real fleet action of the campaign. For the rest of 1942, and for much of 1943, the focus shifted to the Malta convoys, where, for the most part, the Axis contested their passage using aircraft and submarines, rather than surface warships. The Allies made good use of aircraft and submarines too during this period, as British submarines sank *Trento* and *Bande Nere* and damaged *Bolzano* and *Attendolo*, and US aircraft damaged *Gorizia* and sank *Trieste* and *Attendolo*. As a result, by the time of the armistice, as the British were reinforced by new ships and the US Navy, the Italian cruiser force had been reduced to an operational force of just six light cruisers.

ANALYSIS

The actions outlined previously serve to demonstrate that both the Royal Navy and the Regia Marina were still willing to use their cruisers in the time-accustomed manner, fighting surface actions in order to attack or defend convoys, or in support of the main battle fleet. It was rare for cruisers and supporting destroyers to operate alone. For the most part, these light cruisers weren't built for the kind of missions they were usually called upon to perform – defending slow-moving convoys or even screening the battle fleet. Most of the cruisers lacked the armour to allow them to engage in long, drawn-out engagements. The Italians also created their own potential problem by fielding the Zaras almost as if they were miniature capital ships. This policy led to disaster at Matapan. Essentially, though, this restrictive use by both sides meant they were unable to show their true potential. This, of course, didn't mean that they didn't rise to the challenge – the spirited cruiser clashes at Calabria and Spartivento proved that both sides were willing to place their lightly protected cruisers in harm's way if circumstances demanded.

When they did operate independently, albeit with destroyers attached, they were allowed to come into their own. They proved they could be highly effective striking forces. The Malta-based Force K proved this during 1941, while Da Zara's 7th Division in mid-1942, during his operations around Pantelleria, showed its mettle. By then, though, the Regia Marina was suffering from chronic fuel shortages, while at the same time Allied air attacks were on the increase. So, the fuel-guzzling battleships of the fleet were pulled north, and moved from port to port to avoid the bombers, which left Italy's dwindling cruiser force to bear the brunt of naval operations. This in turn meant that despite Da Zara's relative success, the Supermarina preferred to save its cruisers for more defensive missions, such as the protection of convoys. In effect, the Italian fleet was husbanding its limited

An artist's impression of the Battle of Cape Matapan, 28 March 1941. (DeAgostini/Getty Images)

resources, at a time when the Allies, thanks to US intervention, enjoyed an increasing surplus of cruisers.

In terms of the ships themselves, both Britain and Italy were hindered by treaty restrictions, resulting in unbalanced designs. To some extent these were rectified in the Italian Zara and Abruzzi classes, which were as good as any comparable ships in the Royal Navy, and by the British Southamptons and Fijis, which were more balanced designs, with a greatly improved degree of firepower. The Italian ships generally had less underwater protection than their British or Commonwealth counterparts. As a result, several were lost after being hit by a single torpedo. In June 1940, the cruisers of both nations had relatively weak anti-aircraft defences, and both navies took steps to remedy this as the war went on. However, in two other key areas, gunnery and radar, the Regia Marina's cruisers remained inferior to their opponents throughout the war.

When the war began, the Italians realized that the single gun cradles fitted to their cruisers caused the dispersal of their salvos. Several British accounts commented on the accurate ranging of fire from Italian cruisers, but the wide dispersal of their fall of shot. This problem was partially rectified during the war by decreasing muzzle velocity. The guns themselves were well provided for in terms of fire control – the Italian duplex rangefinders and analogue plotting systems worked well enough. In fact, Italian gunnery tended to be very accurate. However, the area in which the Italians remained deficient throughout the war was in radar. By 1941–42, most

During the Battle of Pantelleria in August 1942, Rear Admiral Alberto Da Zara handled his cruisers with commendable skill.

British and Commonwealth cruisers carried some form of surface search and air warning radar, which gave them a significant operational advantage. The Italians only introduced their own version in mid-1943. By then, most British or Commonwealth cruisers were fitted with fire control radars, allowing them to use radar-controlled gunnery, giving them a significant tactical advantage, especially at night.

These problems of design, equipment and function, however, were considerations that only really impacted on the operational and tactical performance of Italy's cruisers. On a more strategic level, they played their part in what was, in some ways, a defensive victory for the Regia Marina. In mid-1940 the Supermarina laid out its plan to control the Central Mediterranean, and so to deny its use to the Royal Navy. Generally, the Italian navy carried out this task, right up until the armistice of September 1943. This meant that for much of the war, the vital British sea route through the Mediterranean was blocked to Allied shipping. In terms of sea power, the British were in the business of sea control – maintaining free passage of the seas. The Italians were in the game of sea denial – preventing the British from exercising this control. It was the cruiser fleets of both sides that fought this battle for control in the Central Mediterranean, but it was the Italians who, until the end, actually achieved their strategic goal.

AFTERMATH

By May 1943, it was clear that the Allies had gained the upper hand in the Mediterranean. The Axis forces in North Africa had surrendered, and Allied planes had begun the regular bombing of Rome. What remained of the Regia Marina had to be moved north, beyond the range of enemy bombers, which exposed Sicily, Sardinia and the Italian mainland to attack. Sure enough, in July the Allies landed in Sicily, and the island was conquered in five weeks. The Italian king had become critical of the war, and supported the growing number of senior Italian figures who sought to end the conflict. On 25 July, the king fired Mussolini, and had him imprisoned. His replacement, Marshal Pietro Badoglio, initiated secret talks with the Allies, which, on 3 September, led to the secret signing of an armistice. With this, the Supermarina began making plans to spirit the Italian fleet away, before it could be seized by the Germans. The armistice was formally announced on 8 September, on the eve of the Allied landing at Salerno. The die was now cast.

Early the following morning, three battleships, three light cruisers and eight destroyers sailed from La Spezia, while other units left from other smaller ports. For instance, an Allied landing force approaching Taranto watched as several powerful Italian warships steamed past them, bound for Malta. They included the *Luigi Cadorna*, as well as two battleships. Those warships which were unable to leave were scuttled or damaged. Most operational warships managed to depart, although they still had to run the gauntlet of German air attacks. The battleship *Roma* was sunk off Sardinia, as were a few small warships, but over the next few days, the bulk of the fleet reached the safety of Allied ports. The majority sailed to Malta, where Vice Admiral Da Zara negotiated their internment with Cunningham. These included six light cruisers – *Luigi Cadorna, Raimondo Montecuccoli, Eugenio di Savoia, Duca d'Aosta, Duca degli Abruzzi* and *Giuseppe Garibaldi*.

On the evening of 11 September, Cunningham signalled the Admiralty: 'Be pleased to inform their Lordships that the Italian battle fleet now lies at anchor under the guns of the fortress of Malta.' This dramatic dispatch marked the end of the long, gruelling campaign. However, there were still a few loose ends to tie up. The heavy cruisers *Bolzano* and *Gorizia* were still under repair in La Spezia, and had to be

The Fiji-class light cruisers *Mauritius*, *Newfoundland* and *Uganda*, pictured while on operations with the Mediterranean Fleet in July 1943. During Operation *Husky* (the Allied invasion of Sicily) they formed part of Support Force East, tasked with shore bombardment of enemy positions.

left behind. The following June, *Bolzano* was sunk by Anglo-Italian human torpedoes, but *Gorizia* was still in La Spezia when the war ended, and she was scrapped two years later. Of the four new Capitani Romani-class cruisers, the *Attilio Regolo* rescued survivors from the *Roma*, then headed to Mahón in Minorca, where she was interned by the Spanish. Two sister ships, *Scipione Africano* and *Pompeo Magno*, also reached Malta – the former carrying Marshal Badoglio and his staff to safety.

On 13 October 1943, the Kingdom of Italy, represented in exile by Marshal Badoglio, declared war on Nazi Germany. The Allies, though, were still distrustful of their former adversaries, and Italy's surviving capital ships continued to be interned, although the two most modern ones were moved to Egypt. Shortly after the declaration of war, *Abruzzi* and *Duca d'Aosta* were fitted with radar and sailed to Freetown in West Africa, under the ensign of the Regia Marina. They were later joined by *Garibaldi*. They remained there until the following April, conducting Atlantic patrols in search of German raiders and blockade runners. Afterwards, together with other Italian cruisers, they were used as fast transports or for Allied gunnery training exercises until the end of hostilities. After the war, several were given to other Allied powers, and *Montecuccoli* became a training ship, but the two Abruzzis remained in Italian service, becoming the core of Italy's new post-war Marina Militare.

As for the Royal Navy, the armistice didn't bring an end to war. The Germans continued to fight, and the Kriegsmarine became increasingly active in the Aegean and Adriatic. British and Commonwealth warships also continued to be lost in Mediterranean waters, including the new cruiser *Spartan,* sunk by a German glide bomb off Anzio in January 1944, and the Force K veteran *Penelope* torpedoed in the same place the following month. A few cruisers remained in the theatre, or were deployed there, and would see further action off northern Italy, in the Aegean or on the southern coast of France. However, for the bulk of the British and Commonwealth cruiser fleet, the war had moved on, and the ships were deployed elsewhere. Many would see out the last year of the war in the Far East as part of the British Pacific Fleet. For their crews, though, many of the men would regard their service in the Mediterranean as the most challenging period of their naval career.

BIBLIOGRAPHY

Bragadin, Marc'Antonio, *The Italian Navy in World War II*, United States Naval Institute, Annapolis MD (1957)

Brescia, Maurizio, *Mussolini's Navy: A Reference Guide to the Regia Marina 1930–45*, Seaforth Publishing, Barnsley (2012)

Campbell, John, *Naval Weapons of World War Two*, Conway Maritime Press, London (1985)

Freidman, Norman, *Naval Radar*, Harper Collins, London (1981)

Friedman, Norman, *British Cruisers: Two World Wars and After*, Seaforth Publishing, Barnsley (2010)

Friedman, Norman, *Naval Firepower: Battleship Guns and Gunnery in the Dreadnought Era*, Seaforth Publishing, Barnsley (2013)

Gardiner, Robert (ed.), *Conway's All the World's Fighting Ships*, 1922–1946, Conway Maritime Press, London (1980)

Gardiner, Robert (ed.), *The Eclipse of the Big Gun: The Warship, 1906–45* (Conway's History of the Ship Series), Conway Maritime Press, London (1992)

Ghiglino, Marco, *Italian Warship Camouflage of World War II*, Seaforth Publishing, Barnsley (2018)

Greene, Jack and Massignani, Alessandro, *The Naval War in the Mediterranean 1940–43*, Chatham Publishing, Rochester (1998)

Grove, Eric, *Sea Battles in Close-Up*, 2 Vols, Ian Allen Ltd, Shepperton (1988–1993)

Heathcote, Tony, *The British Admirals of the Fleet 1734–1995*, Pen & Sword, Barnsley (2002)

Lavery, Brian, *Churchill's Navy: The Ships, Men and Organisation 1939–45*, Conway, London (2006)

Ministry of Information, *The Mediterranean Fleet: Greece to Tripoli – The Admiralty Account of Naval Operations, April 1941 to January 1943*, HMSO, London (1944)

Morris, Douglas, *Cruisers of the Royal and Commonwealth Navies*, Maritime Books, Liskeard (1987)

O'Hara, Vincent, *Struggle for the Middle Sea: The Great Navies at War in the Mediterranean 1940–45*, Conway Maritime Press, London (2009)

Preston, Anthony (ed.), *Jane's Fighting Ships of World War II*, Bracken Books, London (1989). Originally published London, Jane's Publishing Company (1947)

Roberts, John, *British Warships of the Second World War*, Seaforth Publishing, Barnsley (2017)

Roskill, Stephen W., *The War at Sea* (History of the Second World War Series), Vols 1, 2 & 3, HMSO, London (1954)

Sadkovitch, James, *The Italian Navy in World War II*, Praeger Publishing, Santa Barbara CA, (1994)

Thomas, David, *Crete 1941: The Battle at Sea*, André Deutsch Ltd, London (1972)

Whitley, M.J., *Cruisers of World War Two: An International Encyclopaedia*, Arms & Armour Press, London (1995)

Williams, David, *Naval Camouflage 1914–45: A Complete Visual Reference,* Chatham Publishing, London (2001)

Winton, John, *Cunningham: The Greatest Admiral since Nelson*, John Murray Ltd, London (1998)

Wright, Malcolm, *British and Commonwealth Warship Camouflage of WWII*, Vol. 3 (Cruisers, Minelayers and Armed Merchant Cruisers), Seaforth Publishing, Barnsley (2016)

An artist's impression of the light cruiser *Fiji*, namesake of her class, under air attack from the Luftwaffe off Crete on 22 May 1941. She managed to survive a series of twenty air attacks, but then she ran out of ammunition. At that point she was hit by four bombs in two separate attacks, and was sunk with the loss of 241 of her crew.

INDEX

Figures in **bold** refer to illustrations.

Abruzzi class 30–32, 34, 44, 48, 52, 74
Agnew, Captain 'Bill' 63, 64–65
Ajax 11–12, **39**, **49**, 60, 64, **67**, 69
Alberico da Barbiano 27–28, 41, **49**, 62, 65, 68
Alberto da Giussano 27–28, **27**, 41, 62, 65, 68
Arethusa 14–15, **14**, 60
Arethusa class 14–15, 34
Argonaut 19–20, 61
armament
　anti-aircraft 18–22, 48
　fire control 48–50, **51**, 74–75
　gun turrets 44–48, **45**, **47**
　overview 43–48, 74–75
　torpedoes 48
Armando Diaz 27–28, **28**, 62
armour 50–52, 74
Aurora 14–15, 60, **63**, 65

Bartolomeo Colleoni **5**, 27–28, **33**, **36**, **44**, **52**, 62, 66–67
Berwick 9–10, 59, **67**, 68
Birmingham 15–16, 60
Bolzano 22–26, 43–44, 62, 68, 69, 72, 77
Bonaventure 19–20, 61
Breconshire 72
bridges **17**
British Mediterranean Fleet
　command and organization 36–38, 42
　crew and officers 53–56
　fleet composition 58–61
　Force H 16, 36–38, 59, 68
　Force K 12, 34, 41, 63, 64–65, 72, 73
　mission and geographical remit 4–5
Brivonesi, Rear Admiral 65

Cadorna class 27–28
Cairo 20–22, 61, 66, **70–71**
Calabria, Battle of (1940) 67–68
Calcutta 20–22, 61
Caledon 20, 59
Campioni, Vice Admiral Inigo 42, 67–68
Cape Bon, Battle of (1941) 41, 65
Cape Matapan, Battle of (1941) **61**, 69–72, **74**
Cape Spada, action off (1941) **49**
Cape Spada, Battle of (1940) **33**, **36**, **44**, **52**, 66–67
Capetown 20–22, 59
Capitani Romani class 24, 32–33
Carlisle 20–22, 61
Carlisle class 20–22
Casardi, Admiral 66–67
Charybdis 19–20, 61
Cleopatra 19–20, **44**, **46**, 61, **69**, 72
Colombo 20–22, 61
Condottiere class 24, 27–32, 44, 52
Coventry 20, 59
Crete 39, 64, **79**
cruisers
　British and Italian compared 33–34

overview 8–33
performance assessed 5, 73–75
Cunningham, Admiral Sir Andrew **55**
　background and character 55
　and Mediterranean Theatre 36, 38–39, 40, 42, 72, 76–77

Dido 19–20, **46**, **49**, 61, 64, 72
Dido class 19–21, 48
Duca d'Aosta 30–32, **30**, 62, 76, 77
Duca d'Aosta class 30–32, 52
Duca degli Abruzzi 32, **34**, 50, 62, 68, 76, 77

Edinburgh 16, 60
Edinburgh class 16, 17
engine rooms **54**
Eugenio di Savoia 30–32, 50, 62, 66, **70–71**, 76
Euryalus 19–20, **19**, **44**, **46**, 61, 72

Fiji 17–18, 60, **79**
Fiji class 17–18, 34, 74
Fiume 22–24, 26, **38**, **61**, 62, 68, 69

Galatea 14–15, 60
Giovanni delle Bande Nere 27–28, **40**, **46**, 62, 66–67, 72
Giuseppe Garibaldi 32, **32**, **61**, 62, 67–68, 76, 77
Giussano class 27–28, 44
Glasgow 15–16, 60
Gloucester **7**, 15–16, 60, 67, **67**, 69
Gorizia 22–24, 26, **38**, **46**, **58**, 62, 68, 72, 77
Greece 38–39, **39**, 69

Hawkins class 8–9, 11
Hermione 19–20, 61
Hobart 11–14, 60

Iachino, Vice Admiral Angelo 57, **57**, 68, 69, 72

Jamaica 17–18, 60

Kent 9–10, 59
Kent class 9–10, 43, 50–52
Kenya 17–18, **18**, 60

Leander 11–12, 60
Leander class 11–13, 34, 44
Liverpool 15–16, 60, 64, 68
London class 10
London Naval Treaty (1930) 9, 11
London Naval Treaty (1936) 15, 17
Luigi Cadorna 27–28, 62, 76

Malta
　convoys to 38, 65–66, 68, 72
　as fleet base 35–36, **41**, 54–56, 58, 59
　Italian fleet taken to after armistice 76–77
　strategic importance 4–5, 35–36, 42
Manchester 15–16, **54**, 60, 68
Marine Nationale 24, 27, 32–33, 36

Mauritius 17–18, 60, **77**
Montecuccoli class 28–29, 31, **31**, 52
Mussolini, Benito 22, 35, **56**, 76
Muzio Attendolo 28–29, 62, 72

Naiad **18**, 19–21, **21**, 61, 72
Neptune 11–12, **12**, 32, 60, 64, 67–68
Newcastle 15–16, 60, 68
Newfoundland 17–18, 60, **77**
Nigeria 17–18, 60
Norfolk class 10

Operation *Harpoon* (1942) 65–66
Orion 11–12, **49**, **59**, 50, 64, **67**, 68, 69

Pantelleria, Battle of (1942) 41, **70–71**, 75
Penelope 14–15, **51**, 60, 65, 77
Perth 11–14, 60, **67**, 69
Perth class 11–14
Phoebe 19–20, 61
Pola 22–24, 26, **38**, **61**, 62, 68, 69

radar 50, 74–75
Raimondo Montecuccoli 28–29, **29**, 31, **31**, 62, **70–71**, 76, 77
Regia Marina
　command and organization 42
　crews and officers 56–58
　fleet composition 59
　mission and geographical remit 4–5

Scylla 19–20, 61
Sheffield 15–16, **16**, **17**, 60, 68
Sirius 19–20, 61
Sirte, First Battle of (1941) 41
Sirte, Second Battle of (1942) 41, **44**, **46**, 72
Somerville, Vice Admiral Sir James 36–38, 68, **69**
Southampton 15–16, **15**, 60, 68
Southampton class 15–16, 17, 34, 46, **65**, 74
Spartivento, Battle of (1940) **67**, 68
Sydney 11–14, **13**, **44**, 60, 64, 66–67, 68

Taranto 38, **58**
Tiger class 18
Trento **23**
　in action 46, 62, 65, 68, 69, 72
　design 22–25
Trento class 22–25, 43, 52
Trieste 22–25, 26, 62, 65, 68, 69, 72

Uganda 17–18, 60, **77**

Washington Naval Treaty (1922) 8, 22

York **10**, 11, 59, 64
York class 11

Zara 22–24, **24**, 26, **38**, **61**, 62, 69
Zara, Rear Admiral Alberto Da 66, 72, 73, **75**, 76
Zara class 22–24, 26, 34, 43–44, 52, 74